Please Help Me Save My Marriage!

Donald W. Smith

ISBN 978-0-578-99482-6

Scripture quotations are taken from the Holy Bible, King James Version (Public Domain), unless otherwise noted.

Scriptures marked NIV are taken from the NEW INTERNATIONAL VERSION (NIV): THE HOLY BIBLE, NEW INTERNATIONAL VERSION ®. Copyright© 1973, 1978, 1984, 2011 by Biblica, Inc.™. Used by permission of Zondervan

Printed in the United States of America

Table of Contents

"You Cannot Afford A Day Off When It Comes To Your Marriage!"

"Be sober, be vigilant; because your adversary the devil, as a roaring lion, walketh about, seeking whom he may devour," (1 Peter 5:8).

Acknowledgments

To my Friend and Pastor, William C. Keisling. I am *thankful* to God because if it had not been for the Uber ride, I would *never* have met you and became part of the Fort Victory Baptist Church family. I have *truly* been blessed.

To Elder Andre and Jacquelyn Williams, your friendship has been life-changing for me in the last twenty years. Your help with this book and your contribution to help marriages will impact *many* lives and remind people *why* their marriage is worth saving.

To Brother Michael E. and Sister Becky Kline, this book would not have been possible without your help in putting together information to *rescue* marriages on the *brink* of divorce. Your contribution is a blessing to many married couples that *need* to hear your story of *walking* in victory and *trusting* the Lord.

To the Fort Victory Baptist Church family and those who have shown me great love and encouragement. Thank you for all you do to make me better and to assure me that I am loved.

To my readers, I genuinely appreciate your *support* and the *love* you have shown.

Introduction

Please Help Me Save My Marriage! is a widespread cry that needs to be answered with *lasting* and *impactful* results. The days we live in should not surprise the believer because God's Word is very *clear* about what will happen in the Last Days.

We are living in the *Last* Days. We may not save *every* marriage. But, by God's Grace, I will provide answers and help in any way I can with *Hope* for broken hearts. The *mandate* given to me and the *calling* upon my life is to be a Voice of *Hope* and *Compassion*.

Jesus *warned* us what would happen in the Last Days. These are like the days of Noah, the days of marrying and giving in marriage. We do not have a lot of time, and we need to make sure every minute and moment count.

"Redeeming the time, because the days are evil," (Ephesians 5:16).

"But as the days of Noah were, so also will the coming of the Son of Man be. For as in the days before the flood, they were eating and drinking, marrying and giving in marriage, until the day that Noah entered the ark," (Matthew 24:37-38).

The message that people need to *divorce* who they are with so they can find the *right* spouse is a *lie* from the pit of Hell. That was *never* God's plan for marriage. God does not intend for you to use divorce as a *pathway* to your Mr. or Ms. Right. Divorcing someone to find the right one is not God's plan for your marriage. Remember, God *hates* divorce.

I hope that while you are reading this book, you will be *encouraged,* and you will receive *Hope* to press on and trust God to *heal* your marriage. Do not make the mistake many of us have made. Divorcing your spouse *without* trusting God, or doing your part to save it, is *detrimental* in the long run.

I was so deceived as I entered my *second* marriage. Before I divorced my first wife, I prayed and asked God if I could marry again. How duped I was. I did not make any effort to save my first marriage.

The enemy plans to keep your life *off* balance and *trapped* in the same cycle, making the same marital *mistakes*, all the while thinking that divorce will *fix* the problem. Eventually, you look up one day with *several* divorces behind you, yet you are still *unhappy* and *discontent*.

While I was still going through my first divorce, I started getting close to someone. My actions went against Scripture. I was neither fair to the lady I had met nor was it God's will for me to be with her. Yet, I told everyone it was and that once my divorce was finalized, I would marry her. I should have *never* been dating her because I was not a *free* man.

I hope the message in this book will help set you in the *right* direction and give you the tools you need to *rebuild* your marriage. I am *forgiven*. God has *blessed* me to move on. However, I did not align with God's will for my life or marriage during that season.

I hope you *avoid* the mistakes I made.

I *justified* my sins, which is easy to do when you want what you want. I even had a false prophet "confirm" to the lady I was seeing that she was my wife. That was the operation of a *familiar* spirit in agreement with my deception and desire to fulfill my will rather than God's will.

The Bible even warns about this. "Beloved, believe not every spirit, but try the spirits whether they are of God: because many false prophets are gone out into the world," (1 John 4:1).

By allowing the right voices into your life, *your marriage can be saved.*

Chapter 1: The Klines

Do Not Go Through With The Divorce.

I wrote this book to *save* you from going through a divorce. *Please Help Me Save My Marriage!* is a book with a message of *Hope.* There is a *silent* cry across America because many couples are hoping their problems will *fix* themselves. But, unfortunately, many will not admit that they have a problem.

Over the years, I have enjoyed meeting many lovely couples willing to *challenge* each other to make corrections they have agreed on for a healthy marriage and relationship.

My research revealed many couples survive the storms of life because of their faith and a *willingness* to ask each other and themselves the *tough* questions. In this chapter, I write about such a couple, *The Klines.*

Michael and Becky Kline have been married for 35 years. They moved to Texas from the great state of New York as foster parents. They have been united since high school. I guess you would say they were high school sweethearts.

Before I met the Klines, they prayed and sought God's will concerning a new church home to be a part of and serve in. They had visited Fort Victory Baptist Church but had not decided to join. When I first met them, I knew there was something *special* and *unique* about them.

An Answer To Prayer

At the same time, I was praying fervently that The Lord would move upon their hearts to become a part of the ministry. The Lord answered my prayer. Since becoming a part of FVBC, the Klines have demonstrated *unrelenting* commitment. They have made a tremendous difference because of their servant hearts.

The *strength* of their marriage is a great example. We need more examples of strong marriages in our communities. We need to be *willing* to ask couples *tough* questions and be *ready* to receive real answers that will change the destiny of many unions within our community, especially in our churches.

The number of divorces in our churches is a crisis we need to *resolve* through prayer and communication. How many marriages can be *preserved* if the couples in the pews are *willing* to put in the work and the effort?

You can *revive* your marriage. It is my prayer that the message in this book will give you the *courage* to endure. You can learn from the failures and the successes of others. Your marriage should not simply survive but *thrive*. The Klines have been through many storms, yet they have succeeded. Having the right influence in your marriage is *vital* to its success.

The Klines have a story to share that will *direct* you to fight the *right* way with the right *influence* in your life. We always hear that *communication* is the key to a *successful* marriage. That is the barrier Brother Kline wrestled with because he was not a good communicator.

The Turning Point

After going to a couple's retreat, he realized he needed to be a *better* communicator. That was an area of his life he needed to work on to *revive* his marriage. While attending the retreat, he heard other couples share some of the issues they were going through and what helped them move forward.

The heart's desire of the Klines is to help you move forward and have *victory* through *prayer* and your *commitment* to making the necessary changes in your marriage. If you are married or planning on being married, it is imperative to know communication will be *critical*.

This book will help you start in the right direction. Whether you decide to invest a weekend with other couples at a retreat or sit in a counselor's office will depend on what works for you as a couple.

The Klines are very *adamant* about how *several* couple's retreats pointed them in a direction that helped them work through some challenging issues they were facing.

But, unfortunately, you are headed for a *vicious* cycle of failure and discouragement without the correct information and understanding.

The love the Klines had for each other was evident while I interviewed them. Perhaps, you no longer feel the love, so you have decided to *end* your marriage. Please do not allow your feelings to *dictate* your next step.

Sister Becky is *passionate* about helping other couples. She expressed a desire for wives in *struggling* marriages to reach out to her for *support* and *encouragement*. She has a willingness in her heart to help others experience victory the way they did.

Suppose you are both willing to put in the work to *save* your marriage. In that case, there are couples across America with a heart like the Klines, *ready* to walk alongside you and help you through the rough patches in your marriage because your relationship is worth it.

If you are currently in an *abusive* marriage, please put this book down and take the necessary steps to get to a *safe* place. Remember, feelings can get you in trouble.

You may be thinking this is the day your mate will *stop* hitting you. Your life is worth living in safety. Make a move now!

Will The Problem Fix Itself?

From a personal standpoint, I know all too well the *cost* of avoiding the tough questions and what happens when you *hope* the problem will fix itself. However, it is time to have the courage to *ask* tough questions. I know it will not be easy, but it will be *beneficial* for your marriage in the long run.

I do not care how many *easy* buttons you are sold in life; some roads you travel will be a little rocky. But, you need the *correct* answers to make it through. The Klines are willing to *share* with you what helped *strengthen* their marriage.

Decide to *unload* your heart and *share* what is eating away at you. But, first, you must be *honest* about where you have failed—*kick pride to the curb*. If not, pride will continue to be in the way until you are willing to admit you have a problem and need help.

Never give up or think no one cares.

Couples like the Klines care. That is why they shared how they made it through the *tough* times. Talking to the right person will make a difference. Perhaps you do not know who to talk to at this point or maybe have no one to turn to for help. Keep reading so you can have the courage to make it through.

Identify Your True Friends

Think about this for a moment. You may have friends to talk to who *agree* with you, yet you still feel *empty* and *unfulfilled* after the conversation with them. A true friend will speak *truth* into your life, even if it means *disagreeing* with you. The correct information will help you.

The Scripture below is very clear about your destiny if you allow pride to *dictate* your steps. "Pride goeth before destruction, and an haughty spirit before a fall," (Proverbs 16:18).

Humble yourself!

Reach out to Jesus Christ. His Love will give you *Hope*. Accepting The Lord in your heart and life makes the difference.

The Klines message is that if you are willing to go the *extra* mile and *admit* you need help, you are halfway to seeing your marriage *healed*. Deep down, I believe that is what you desire. Otherwise, you would not be reading this book. So keep reading because you are at the *crossroads* and need answers to produce results that will be beneficial in the long run.

Having the right influence is *critical*. If people always agree with you when they know you are wrong, how does that benefit you in the long run?

Earlier, I mentioned couple's retreats and counseling from professionals. Remember, many pastors have the training to help you as well. The Klines have shared a great deal about the couple's retreats and how blessed they have been by the results they have seen each time they would attend.

The Klines recommend couple's retreats because those have been instrumental in helping them and many other couples. In addition, each retreat was a learning experience, providing them the tools they needed to keep their marriage strong.

A Toolbox For Marriage

Marriage ministry is *needed* in the Body of Christ. When you are around like-minded individuals, they will help your marriage, and you will find what works for you.

If you are around someone who *always* agrees with you and *never* speaks the truth when you need to hear it, you will never receive anything from them that will help you in the long run.

Brother Kline is a *brother* among brothers. His love for the Body of Christ and his willingness to help others is shown through his *commitment* to serve. This determination is *evident* at his job and in the community where he lives.

I can say the same for Becky Kline as well. She has a *heart* for the hurting, and her commitment as a foster parent can be seen in the love she shows the kids they are taking care of. I know the extent the Klines have gone to bring families back together. They demonstrate that same spirit of caring when it comes to marriages as well.

You Are Not Alone

Please note that throughout America, God has people like the Klines *willing* to be a friend to a hurting couple, with no hidden agenda, ready to *pray* with you and help you *save* your marriage. So pray and ask God to *allow* the right individuals to come into your life so you can see the *benefit* of having the right influence and guidance.

Discovering that you need to change your life to salvage your marriage can be a *touchy* subject. However, if you are *stuck* on a hamster wheel of repeatedly marrying and divorcing, you need to go *back* to the drawing board and see where you failed. I have been married *twice*. It has been *five* years since my last divorce, yet, I am not sure if I will be married *again*.

The Klines are very *adamant* about how important it is to put in the work and effort in *finding* what will work for your marriage, coming to an *agreement* with your spouse, and moving forward with a *unified* decision on the *next* steps each of you shall take, both *personally* and *corporately*.

The Power of Agreement

Understanding the Scriptures below is instrumental in helping you *recognize* and *appreciate* the *power* of agreement. "Can two walk together, except they be agreed?" (Amos 3:3).

"Again I say unto you, That if two of you shall agree on earth as touching any thing that they shall ask, it shall be done for them of My Father Which is in heaven," (Matthew 18:19).

These scriptures illustrate God's plan for your *life*, your *marriage*, and the power of *agreement*. If you are looking for results, you have to *stop* making excuses. Excuses pave an *endless* road to *nowhere* and keep you on a *deserted* street of *hopelessness*.

The keys the Klines share are intended to *help* you and give you *Hope* so that you can *save* your marriage. At the end of the book, I share additional information that provides you with further directions and instructions.

"Change Me Instead of Changing Him"

These were Becky Kline's words of what The Lord led her to do. "Lord, change me so I can be a better person and wife to my husband."

As a result, God changed *his* heart as well. Today, their marriage is a shining example of what happens when *two* individuals decide that God is their *only* hope in saving their marriage.

Brother Kline *thought* he was saved and *knew* the Lord. There is a difference between *thinking* and *knowing* you are saved. Brother Kline knew he *needed* the Lord in his life. When he realized his first act of faith in *accepting* Christ in his heart was not the final step, he discerned how much *more* of The Lord he *wanted* in his life. There was still more to experience after that first step. He came home one day and told Becky they *needed* to go to Church.

Between the two of them, Michael was the *first* one saved. After that, his prayer was that Becky would come to salvation as well. What a lesson he learned in *trusting* Christ to do what he could not do. While they were shopping at Walmart, Michael asked Becky a question concerning life after death. Right there and then, he knew he *had* to trust God to save Becky.

A Change of Heart

You cannot *force* salvation and change on anyone. I wish I learned this lesson *during* my first marriage. I stood in God's way concerning the salvation of my former wife. As of the writing of this book, I am not sure if she has come to a place of salvation. So, I *constantly* keep her in prayer that she would *accept* Christ in her heart.

During my first marriage, I did a terrible job of trusting God to do whatever was needed. I was *impatient* for things to change and all that did was create *problems* for my first wife and me. I wrote this book so you can learn what my failure *cost* me. Be quick to shun pride and self-righteousness.

If this chapter addresses your situation in life, it behooves me to encourage you to take in all that is being shared to help you make it. Brother Kline learned early on that he needed to *trust* God to *save* Becky.

"For the unbelieving husband is sanctified by the wife, and the unbelieving wife is sanctified by the husband: else were your children unclean; but now are they holy," (1 Corinthians 7:14).

"Husbands, love your wives, even as Christ also loved the church, and gave Himself for it;" (Ephesians 5:25).

Third Wheel

If you will have a third wheel in your decision, it is crucial to have someone who will not always agree with you. There is a tendency for us to *want* people who *understand* and *agree* with us, whether it is beneficial for us or not. Even the Klines had *both* good and bad influences.

The third wheel will either *help* or *hinder* you. If you are a believer, you need *firm* believers in your life. Be careful who you share your *hurts* with.

The Kline family has the heart to help others. Maybe you have been given evil *counsel*, have a poor *understanding*, and see no way out but divorce. The Klines want you to know you *can* make it. Considering how *busy* their lives are, you may be wondering how in the world can they do it and *keep* their marriage going strong. All of us have been challenged, and each day we have something pulling at us. *Yet, we keep going.*

I have been invited to the Kline's home several times, and I have been so blessed by their marriage and their *commitment* to serve others.

Spiritual Needs

As many believers tend to do, we *overlook* spiritual needs in our household. Such was my case. During my interview with Brother Kline, he gave me a lot to think about. I began to reflect on my first marriage and wondered if I ever considered the needs of my household. It was *all about me* and what I believed God was *calling me to do* at the time.

One of the main reasons the Klines were looking for a church home was because Brother Kline finally saw that the spiritual need in his family was going *unsatisfied* and *unaddressed*. As you read this book, perhaps you realize you have been overlooking the spiritual needs in your family. I pray that your spiritual eyes would be *open* to the needs in their lives as well.

The Klines made a *promise* to each other that they would do whatever was *right* to keep their marriage *strong* and not compromise along the way. Their *victory* resided in *correctly* applying the right information. Compromises only create *deeper* problems.

If the hurt is not dealt with, it only leads to more *severe* troubles. Therefore, do not allow hurt to *control* the decisions you make for the next phase of your marriage. Now is the time to be on guard and *prayerful* at all times. Making the *wrong* decisions will only take you *further* away from each other. That is what the *enemy* of your soul is after.

The Ugly Face of Divorce

It is important to know you *need* help. The earlier you *admit* what you need, the sooner you will *start* moving forward. Divorce does not need to be the *end-point* of your decisions. Let Christ be at the *center* of your relationship.

I asked Sis Kline, "What did you do to keep your relationship moving forward?

She replied, "Habit!"

She went on to explain that going to church was a *big* part of their life. There were times they went to church while *mad* at each other. They would *hear* the Word of God. The Lord would *speak* to them. Brother Kline would then *comfort* his wife, "We are going to make it."

Each time they would leave the church a little *stronger* and *encouraged* to press forward. They knew to go to church and *seek* the Lord. No matter what it looked like, God would give them an answer that would *fortify* them to continue onward. "I can do all things through Christ Which strengtheneth me," (Philippians 4:13).

Older Women

I asked Sister Kline, "Were there any older women that encouraged you to love your husband and be strong in The Lord?"

She answered, "Most of them would talk badly about their husbands." But, unfortunately, those conversations did not help her.

She *refused* to allow that kind of talk to *cloud* her faith and make her feel a certain way toward her husband. How many of our decisions have been influenced by *wrong* conversation and character *assassination* that never gave us hope or drew us closer to God's will for our lives and marriage?

The verse below is so clear on what is needed in the Body of Christ. So many ministries have implemented this approach to help married couples. "That they may teach the young women to be sober, to love their husbands, to love their children,"(Titus 2:4).

Brother Kline said a married couple may not *always* agree with each other. At times they need to *table* an issue and come back to it *later* when they can find a place of *compromise* that will keep the *peace* and *harmony* between them.

Does Encouragement Matter?

I asked Brother Kline, "How important was encouragement to you?"

He responded, "Very important!" He went on to acknowledge that Becky kept him encouraged. He has always been *thankful* for her love and the *genuine* way she would keep him built up. They both agree it goes both ways.

Michael and Becky Kline may not *know* you, but they pray for you because each book purchase denotes someone *reaching* for prayer. Prayer warriors are standing in the gap for your marriage. I update them with the number of books purchased because each purchase represents *someone* looking for answers. You are not a stranger to us. We are ministers that care about your wellbeing and marriage.

Chapter 2: The Williams

A Love That Was Found.

You may be like many other couples, where it all *started* with a love story. Yet, now you may be going through *turmoil* and *looking* for an answer to *save* your marriage. Maybe Today is a *hard* day for you, and you cannot even begin to think about Tomorrow.

As I think back, I can confess I *needed* answers. God's Word was available to read and *apply* as a guide. I can remember the day I had to *stand* before the judge. I recall him declaring us *divorced*. Yet, I was still in love with her no matter what had happened to us. I hope you are reading this book looking for answers because you still *want* your marriage to work.

With that in mind, let me tell you about the Williams. They met in passing at a Mardi Gras event, not knowing that they would become *more* than strangers one day. Jacquelyn did not know Andre had giving her a lot of thought and *wanted* to meet her again. However, she lived in her world, not thinking about marriage because she was divorced and still *healing* from the abusive relationship. If anything, she had made up her mind *never* to marry again.

When a *tragic* relationship happens in your life, it brings experience and *shapes* your mind and desires for future decisions. If you are not careful, that *tarnished* relationship will frame a *wrong* impression of everyone you meet thereafter.

The best way to handle the past is to *learn* from it, yet not allow it to keep you from moving forward. The pain of the past will decide for you if you do not *educate* yourself and be aware of what the enemy may use to keep you from *seeing* the hand of God moving on your behalf.

Are All Men The Same?

Jacquelyn had made up in her mind that all men were the same. But, little did she know, all men are *not* the same. Given time, she would learn that, because her heart began to open up.

God began to deal with Elder Williams about how Jacquelyn would be his wife, even though there was an age difference. Her first marriage had lasted 19 years. Jacquelyn decided she would have *fun* with life and *never* marry again, but God had *different* plans for her. Finally, the time came, and they met at a house party.

Elder Williams expressed his desire to be a part of her life. At this time, he was in a backslidden state, and she had not yet committed her life to Christ. So many marriages start on the *wrong* side of the road, yet God can take a couple from where they *failed* and bring them to a place of *honor* in life.

Jacquelyn never wanted to be in a *committed* relationship. She informed him that it was best for him not to fall in love with her because she would *hurt* him, and it would never work out. However, he remained *humble* because he wanted more of her in his life. He treated her like a queen, yet she *resisted* falling in love, remembering the pain of her past hurts.

It Happened...She *Fell* In Love

Jacquelyn still had anger in her heart that needed to be dealt with. Before my second marriage, I harbored anger in my heart that I had not resolved. I was not healed of it. Yet, I married again, carrying all that baggage.

Whatever happens in your marriage, good or bad, *starts* in your heart. That is why it is essential to *face* the hurt. If you do not, your pain will *decide* for you. Before you know it, you are divorced. Your life does not need to end up that way. There is Hope. You can have a *better* outcome in your marriage.

Jacquelyn did not desire to love anybody, *especially* Elder Williams, because she did not know how. Yet, she fell in love with him. Even though he was nothing like her past, it took her some time to see how *blessed* she was to have someone like him in her life who treated her like a queen.

Your hurt can *hinder* you from seeing the good in someone. All you see in your marriage is *undesirable* and *unpleasant*, so you want *out* because of the pain. You are not alone. In many marriages, the past *controls* how couples respond to hurt and disappointment.

Jacquelyn had been in the same situation. She had felt her *only* option was divorce. Now that she was divorced, Jacquelyn had no desire to marry again because she *assumed* all men were the same. She has since learned that the *answer* is Christ. She received Him as her Savior, and because of that, her *whole* household was saved.

Are You Afraid To Love Again?

Jacquelyn was *afraid* to love again because she did not want to *risk* another *abusive* marriage. She put up walls. It was not until she had a *change* of heart that she saw she was in a *safe* place.

If you are *full* of hurt and pain, it will be hard for you to *recognize* hope. It took the *healing* of her heart for her to see how much God *loved* her and wanted to *change* her destiny. She admitted that Elder Williams was loving and kind toward her; however, she tried to control everything.

That gave her a sense of *power* over her life and Elder Williams as well. She was *hurting*. She did not believe she could *love* anyone anymore.

The change began to happen before she *accepted* Christ as her personal Savior. God was *already* dealing with her heart and giving her hope. With the right help, you too can make it.

You Can Save Your Marriage

Elder Williams did not know that someone was *sharing* the Plan of Salvation with Jacquelyn behind the scenes. She came home one day and *announced* she had *accepted* Christ. Conviction had set in, and Jacquelyn knew they could not continue living the way they had been. She knew he had to move *out*, not knowing God had been dealing with his heart as well.

They both *recognized* The Lord was at work in their hearts. They had pain and asked God to take it away. Divorce is a far cry from the way God takes away the pain in marriage. It is the will of God for your marriage to be *healed*. If you pray, God will bring the *right* individual into your life to *help* you. All you need to do is *ask*, and He will *answer* you.

Before their marriage, Elder Williams and Jacquelyn were already operating in a place where God's mercy was available to them. Yet, Elder Williams never gave up on her.

When she asked him to move out, he responded, "Are you crazy, because I do not want to lose you?" He continued, "Set a date because I want you to become my wife!"

They were married three months later. Now, after 26 years of marriage, they have a testimony of how The Lord can *keep* a marriage together.

What Do You Admire In Them?

Elder Williams stated he *admired* Jacquelyn's stand for holiness and wanting to get things *right* before marriage, just as she got past all the abuse in her heart and realized he was the right man for her. However, she could not see the good until The Lord *healed* her heart.

You will not see any good and hope in your marriage until you *forgive* and are *healed* of the hurt that is in your heart. Until you *admit* your part in the failure of your marriage and *repent* to each other, history will continue to *repeat* itself.

Love Does Not Give Up

Jacquelyn shared with me that she was a *nagging* woman. She was always looking at his faults. She was like a dripping fountain leaking *abusive* words toward him. Yet, he kept *reacting* with love.

"A continual dropping in a very rainy day and a contentious woman are alike," (Proverbs 27:15).

"A soft answer turneth away wrath: but grievous words stir up anger," (Proverbs 15:1).

Jacquelyn asked Elder Williams why he put up with her crazy talk toward him. He informed her, "Love does not run. I love you, and love does not give up."

"And above all things have fervent charity among yourselves: for charity shall cover the multitude of sins," (1 Peter 4:8).

Love *covers*.

Challenging seasons are a good time for you and your spouse to cover each other with love. However, be careful who you talk to about each other because it could *hinder* you both from moving forward.

When I look back at my life, I realize I should not have been *pacified* talking only with the individuals that *agreed* with me. Instead, I needed people to *challenge* me, to better understand my marriage, and encourage me to *pursue* what The Lord could do to help us.

I have been married twice. If my first wife and I had fought a *good* fight and *never* given up, we would be *together* today because her will would have given in to God's will. I thought I was in the will of God because I met someone while going through my first divorce. I was *still* married.

My thinking was way off. I was not *free* to pursue someone else. I was *out* of the will of God. Seventeen years later, I suffered the *consequences* of that decision. God will never *sanction* a relationship out of His will. I was *already* married.

I cannot believe I even prayed about it. I was a heretic and out of the will of God. I told everybody God had sent me my second wife. A false prophet called me and *lied* to me about my first wife. How sad and devastating to know I was in my flesh when I took that stand.

A Word of Encouragement

Do not make the mistakes I made. Instead, *learn* from my failures and seek out *godly* counsel so The Lord will be *pleased* with your decision. Go to God and ask him to put you in *remembrance* of why you both fell in love in the first place. Ask God to reveal why you felt that way.

After the Williams got married, they began to have problems they never encountered while shacking up and living *outside* the will of God. Elder Williams can remember going to bed fussing and waking up in turmoil.

He asked God to teach him how to love his wife despite what she was saying to him. He would take Jacquelyn's hand and say, "I love you." The Lord helped them to *remain* strong. Today, they look back and know it was God's grace that brought them over to victory.

How To Avoid Having A Bad Fight?

1. Talk about *why* it all happened

2. Communicate with each other, which is the *key* to saving your marriage.

3. Do not *allow* emotions to take over.

Words of Wisdom

Initially, Elder Williams was the one working hard to keep everything together before Jacquelyn came around. You may be the one who is holding the door of communication open. I will end this chapter with these *Words of Wisdom From The Williams*.

Elder Andre Williams' words of wisdom:

- Every marriage deserves a *second* chance.
- Look at the years you both have *invested*.
- Do not look at the *negatives*.
- You need to *want* your marriage to work.
- Fight *fair* with each other.

Lady Jacquelyn Williams' words of wisdom.

- Think about how you both *first* met.
- Seek God for *healing* in the marriage.
- Believe in each other *again*.
- If you want your marriage to *work*, seek godly help and counsel.

Chapter 3: Making The Wrong Turn

The Fall Was Not God's Intention.

God never intended for Adam and Eve to experience The Fall or for us to be *shackled* with the consequences of it. This chapter addresses why we take *wrong* turns in life and end up *outside* of what God intended for us. Since the fall of humanity, it is in our nature to *blame* each other for our failures. That is why there is a high *rate* of divorce and a large number of *casualties* who have fallen by the wayside.

God's plan was for Adam to make the *right* choices in life and eat *every* tree in The Garden, *except* the Tree of the Knowledge of Good and Evil (Genesis 2:17). God *permitted* him to eat of every tree except one. He knew what God said would happen if he disobeyed.

Where would we be today if Adam and Eve had *only* eaten of the right tree? Please keep in mind, what is most important is an *obedient* heart and a *desire* to do the right thing according to God's plan. The Scriptures below are very clear about what happens when we are disobedient.

"And the Lord God commanded the man, saying, Of every tree of the garden thou mayest freely eat: but of the tree of the knowledge of good and evil you shall not eat, for in the day that you eat of it you shall surely die," (Genesis 2:16-17).

The Garden

God created The Garden *after* Adam.

God created Adam *outside* The Garden from the dust of the ground, then breathed life into him. Next, God placed man in The Garden to take care of it. In The Garden, God made Eve from Adam's rib, and they both had *clear* instructions on their responsibilities.

It was never God's plan for you to be a robot. You were to be a *willing* and *obedient* servant who *loves* Him and desires to *please* Him in all you do. Remember, the serpent *tempted* Eve. Just as is needed with men today, Adam should have had a godly backbone and taken a *stand* to be who God was calling him to be.

All across America today, there is an *attack* on men's masculinity: in homes, in government, more so in Hollywood, and churches. The spirit of Jezebel is showing up in all parts of society, *assaulting* leadership in the pulpit and the home.

Do you find yourself *continually* making wrong turns in life? Each time it happens, you tell yourself you will do *better* and make the necessary changes to *improve* your life. However, before you see a better *outcome* for a better life, something must change *inside* you.

The Fall of man started with a *decision*.

Unfortunately, Adam did not realize how far-reaching his decision would be or the results it would bring.

Wrong turns affect *all* of us.

Learning From Failure

What can you *learn* from the failure of Adam and Eve? One of the first things, it was *never* God's plan for things to fall in this direction. But, thank God, He had a plan to *restore* you to a relationship with Him by sending His Son, *the Last Adam.*

Through Him, you will *win* in the end if you *repent* and have a change of heart that only God can do in you as you *accept* Christ as your Lord and Savior. At the end of this book, I share how to *receive* Him.

God's Word teaches that Adam was with Eve, but *nothing* happened until he *ate* the fruit. So why did something happen *after* he ate it? Why did he *disobey* God outright?

"For as by one man's disobedience many were made sinners, so by the obedience of One shall many be made righteous. Moreover the law entered, that the offence might abound. But where sin abounded, grace did much more abound: That as sin hath reigned unto death, even so might grace reign through righteousness unto eternal life by Jesus Christ our Lord," (Romans 5:19-21).

When you take wrong turns in life and make decisions without God, you get *off* track and become *discouraged* with life. It is important not to *lose* hope because God is faithful to help you if you *ask* Him. God loves you and does not want you to continue to butt heads with your mate in despair. It is my hope you will *learn* from my mistakes and failures. I am willing to *admit* my shortcomings in trying to do things my way so that you can learn from them.

You can *rekindle* your love for the one you once loved. Remember how *much* you loved them before. Forgive them. Returning to love is possible if you both make the decision *together* and *learn* from what happened. You will both gain so much more, and your marriage will be *stronger* than before.

"I can do all things through Christ Which strengtheneth me," (Philippians 4:13).

Turning to God will give you the hope you need *beyond* what you may currently comprehend. It is God's will for you to make it in life and marriage. God is not your enemy. The verse below reveals God's desire for your life.

"Now unto Him that is able to do exceeding abundantly above all that we ask or think, according to the power that worketh in us," (Ephesians 3:20).

This verse gives me hope because I am ready to *meet* someone. I hope that I do not make a wrong turn again. If I *trust* God and His plans for me, I know I will not. I hope you will do the same!

Chapter 4: Why A Woman Finds It So Hard To Forgive

A Woman's Pain.

As I was conducting interviews for this chapter, I braced myself for what some ladies might share concerning why it is *hard* for a woman to forgive. I am careful not to put all women in this category. Some ladies have the honor of forgiving *quickly* and loving as if *nothing* ever happened. Later, we will examine what makes them so unique and admired by others.

The challenges a woman faces each day after being hurt can make it hard for them to forgive. What once gave her hope has turned into a bridge to *hopelessness*, causing her deep *discouragement*. It seems there is no hope of even making it.

I intended to interview a couple together, but the lady convinced me otherwise. She adamantly maintained that if I brought her husband into the conversation, he would probably leave her. He was full of pride and had chosen not to learn what it would take to be the husband he needed to be.

He was a *leader* in the community and attended church *regularly* for his spiritual *growth* and to *build* his faith. Sometimes, I wonder *why* we go to church and praise God yet leave the *same* way we went. That is one of the many reasons why a woman finds it so *hard* to forgive.

The church is full of *wounded* individuals in marriages where they are just going through the motions. This tragedy is being experienced from the *pulpit*, where the message is presented to the people, all the way to the *usher*, who stands and greets everyone with a smile, welcoming them to the worship service. Living by faith and trusting God to do what you cannot do will *change* your heart.

The Church Leader's Struggle

Church leaders need to stand up and address the need for healing in the Body of Christ. One main reason a leader finds it *hard* to talk with someone, even if they sense something is wrong, is fear the person will become *offended*. This has left many godly marriages stranded in *difficult* places. The couples *desire* to forgive and walk in love, but they need *help* getting there.

If leaders do not address this issue, many more marriages will end up in Divorce Court as the *preferred* remedy for their hurt. Many people are in their second or third marriage after using divorce as the *solution* for the problems of their previous marriage. Divorce is a challenging subject to tackle. However, with *guidance* from God's Word and the *comfort* of The Holy Spirit, leaders can make a difference.

Numerous godly women are married to men who cannot wait to arrive at church with their masks on to make everyone think all is well at home. These messages *confuse* women concerning their man's love for The Lord because their actions behind closed doors do not line up with God's Word.

Stop Going Through The Motions

If just one marriage is in trouble, we need to be ready to offer help because the *"Please Help Me Save My Marriage!"* cry is all around us. It is time for couples to stop going through the motions as if everything is okay and they do not need any help.

In my first book, *Forgive Who? How A Man Can Forgive His Ex-Wife And Move On With Life*, I hoped to *expel* the myth that all men are cruel. Some have been *hurt* and railroaded into terrible marriages. My goal in writing this book was to discuss the tricky subject and what we can do to keep marriages *free* from the claws of divorce.

What causes a woman to harbor unforgiveness yet go through each day like everything is okay? A godly woman will *keep* her focus on the Lord. Knowing this will *awaken* your heart to how God's Word can bring you, as a woman, to a place of *freely* forgiving your husband of all the hurt and pain he caused in your life. You can experience the victory you have only in Christ.

You Were Not Created For Abuse

I want to be clear. It is not God's will for you to be *roadkill*, to be beaten upon verbally or physically. If you are being abused or experiencing domestic violence, please pack your clothes, and get out before it is too late to recover.

Mental abuse is as *dangerous* as verbal and physical abuse. God never created you to be beaten up. Get out so you can think more clearly and know what your next step will be.

If you are *struggling* with hope, keep reading now that you have made it this far. After reading earlier chapters, especially the one about the Klines, remember they suggested marriage retreats. The Klines acknowledged how *interacting* with other couples and listening to them *enabled* them to gain a great deal of *insightful* information as they navigated through the *challenging* seasons in their marriage.

Consider the wife who truly *loves* her husband and *desires* for her marriage to *heal*. Unfortunately, her husband may be very *selfish*, thinking only of himself. That keeps her wondering if the marriage is going to make it through their struggles. His demeanor and treatment of her do not give her much confidence.

A Damaging Love Language

You may find it hard to believe; however, the way he *treats* her is *his* love language. He loves being able to *control* every moment and facet of their life. Nevertheless, is this the way someone should love? *Absolutely not.*

How do you help a couple in this situation? The husband is *unapproachable.* There is a segment of women who are *stuck* in this very situation and desire counseling. They need avenues and solutions that would bring them hope and encouragement.

Whether you are a believer or an unbeliever, only God can help you do what you cannot do in your strength. Yes! God *expects* you to forgive because His Word is very clear about the *power* of forgiving someone and how it *frees* you from living in bondage.

"Or despisest thou the riches of His goodness and forbearance and longsuffering; not knowing that the goodness of God leadeth thee to repentance?" (Romans 2:4).

This verse is very clear about what happens in our heart when we *think* about the goodness of God, *know* how much God loves us, and how *important* it is to forgive.

Is There A Limit To Forgiveness?

You may be asking how *many* times should you forgive for the *same* slip-up. Jesus addressed that same concern.

"Then came Peter to Him, and said, Lord, how oft shall my brother sin against me, and I forgive him? till seven times? Jesus saith unto him, I say not unto thee, Until seven times: but, Until seventy times seven," (Matthew 18:21-22).

Only God's Love can *help* you forgive and strengthen you while trusting Him for the victory. God will give you the Grace you need to be able to stand *firm* in His Love.

"And blessed is he, whosoever shall not be offended in Me," (Matthew 11:6).

God's Word is very clear about forgiving someone. To forgive does not mean the person who hurt you will not suffer the *consequences* of what they carried out against you. You do not need to *execute* the punishment you feel they *deserve*.

You forgive them!

God forgave *you*, and His Love will continue to reach out from your heart as long as you walk according to His Word. That is why you should forgive at *all* times. Remember, God's Love will *empower* you to forgive and walk in *freedom*. Walking in His Love helps us to become *more* like Christ.

"Dearly beloved, avenge not yourselves, but rather give place unto wrath: for it is written, Vengeance is Mine; I will repay, saith the Lord," (Romans 12:19).

Check Your Baggage

You are not *designed* to carry hurt and bitterness. That only makes you sour and *hardens* your heart. You want to be able to *hear* the cry of the hurting. Love *always* finds a way. God loves you so much that His Love found a way to bring you *back* to Him by sending His Only Begotten Son to *pay* a price you could not pay.

God will *strengthen* you to carry out His purpose in your life. In Christ, you *are* an overcomer. The enemy will attempt to make you think *nothing* can and will ever change. Rejoice in the fact that you *are* an overcomer.

"For whatsoever is born of God overcometh the world, And this is the victory that overcometh The world, even our faith," (1 John 5:4).

The world would teach you it is best to *hold* the hurt *against* the one who hurt you. But, on the other hand, God leads you to *forgive* to be *free* and avoid living in bondage.

"If the Son therefore makes you free ye shall be free indeed," (John 8:36).

You are *free* from the grips of the enemy whose only task is to keep you in *bondage* to your past. God's Love comes to set you free and keep you growing in it. Regarding what the Lord will do in your heart to be more like Christ and forgive, the sky is the limit.

Are you walking the *tightrope* of life, living in *fear*, and looking for answers? Are you holding on to Hope because of Christ's Love? I wrote this book for you.

My goal was to give you Hope in your marriage as you trust God to *touch* your mate's heart and bring a change that will *bless* your home.

It is time for leaders in the Body of Christ to address this complex subject of marriage because it is a silent cry coming from the hearts of the hurting, and that cry is, *Please Help Me Save My Marriage!*

Chapter 5: Are You Struggling To Forgive?

The Mountain Called Forgiveness.

Forgiveness is a challenging subject to tackle because you may have had *different* experiences handling day-to-day problems from the next person. In addition, forgiving someone will be *influenced* by the kind of environment you grew up in and the trauma you may have faced.

You relate based on *your* experiences. But, as I share mine, we can have a meeting of the minds and hearts somewhere in the middle. As I grew up, my father spent a lot of time *away* from home because he was a club owner on the south side of Fort Worth in Texas. I might add, I found out this later on in life.

I remember coming home from school and my mother saying to me, "Well, your father will probably not be home for a while. So you are going to need to be the man of the house and help me."

That was our life for a *long* season.

When my father eventually came home, my mother *always* treated him with love and respect. I never heard them arguing about *why* he stayed away at times. I did not realize until later that I was being *trained* for my life today.

My mother walked in love and never talked to me about my father *behind* his back. She never uttered what he was doing to her *outside* their marriage. So my *first* experience of seeing someone walking in forgiveness was with my mother. She *protected* my father's character, even though he was not a man of Honor at the time.

I Brought My Paycheck Home

I worked at Cook Children's Hospital washing dishes. I brought my paycheck home to my parents. I never thought about *keeping* my check, letting you know how *different* young people were then from young people today. No one ever *told* me to bring my check home. Instead, I gave it to my parents because, for some reason, it was *instilled* in me to do just that. I look back now and realize The Lord had me in a place to help my parents during a *challenging* time I did not know.

My mother had to walk in love because she *wanted* their marriage to survive, even if it meant her feeling *less* than important to him at the time. You are probably wondering *how* she could walk in forgiveness. My mother was a *prayer* warrior, and she *loved* God with all her heart.

The reason it is *hard* for many to forgive is because of their *weak* relationship with The Lord. God's Love is all about *forgiving* those who have hurt you or let you down.

Have You Been Forgiven?

How many times *will* God forgive you? How many times *has* God forgiven and *reinstated* you as if nothing ever happened?

Let's look at the question the Apostle Peter asked. Many scholars believe Peter had an issue with someone, and he wanted to know how many times he should forgive them.

"Then came Peter to Him, and said, Lord, how oft shall my brother sin against me, and I forgive him? till seven times? Jesus saith unto him, I say not unto thee, Until seven times: but, Until seventy times seven," (Matthew 18:21-22).

How many times have you been forgiven? From this verse, it is clear that forgiveness has *no limits*. The only way you can walk in this kind of forgiveness will depend on your relationship with God. Therefore, when I talk with individuals who say they love God but *cannot* forgive, my very word to them is, "How can you love God who you have not seen, yet you see your brothers and sisters every day and cannot forgive them?"

"If a man say, I love God, and hateth his brother, he is a liar: for he that loveth not his brother whom he hath seen, how can he love God Whom he hath not seen?" (1 John 4:20).

You cannot love God with *all* your heart and walk in unforgiveness. That is *impossible* to do because the Love of God is shed abroad in your heart.

"And hope maketh not ashamed; because the love of God is shed abroad in our hearts by the Holy Ghost Which is given unto us," (Romans 5:5).

As You Do, So He Does

How you forgive is a direct correlation with how God will forgive you. "So likewise shall My Heavenly Father do also unto you, if ye from your hearts forgive not every one his brother their trespasses," (Matthew 18:35).

Peter was hoping for an outcome that would fit his *preferred* course of action, but The Lord was very clear about how we should forgive each other, never *holding* bitterness in our hearts. Thus, my relationship with others is a *direct* correlation of my connection to God and His Love that is in my heart.

My mother *loved* God with *all* her heart, and she was able to walk out her faith and *forgive* my father. She loved him when he was not even loveable. The Love of God *covers* a multitude of sin. That is precisely what my mother demonstrated. She covered my father. I never knew what was going on with them until I was old enough to form my own opinion.

If it is *hard* for you to forgive, and you do not want bitterness to take over your heart, ask God to search your heart and *expose* the cause.

"Search me, O God, and know my heart: try me, and know my thoughts: And see if there be any wicked way in me, and lead me in the way everlasting," (Psalm 139:23-24).

Many Pay This Costly Price

You may be wondering why I am sharing so many verses from The Bible. First, it is *essential* to know what The Lord is saying concerning forgiveness. Second, it is crucial to understand how *vital* forgiveness is for *fulfilling* His will in our lives; we *love* one another and *walk* in forgiveness.

Neglecting to walk in love and forgiveness will *hinder* your prayers and blessings in your life. A hindrance to your prayer is too *steep* a price to pay because of anger in your heart toward your neighbor. The more you love God and His Word, the more you will be *changed* into the image of Christ. Only then will you see the Glory of God in your life.

My mother loved God and knew *saving* her marriage was going to take *much* prayer. I found out later she had a prayer chain going for the family. Eventually, my father got saved and *left* the street to become a believer in Christ, *serving* The Lord for the *rest* of his life.

I am so glad my mother did not give up on my father because I may have been pulled into that club life and become a club owner today instead of serving The Lord with all my heart. The commitment my mother made for walking in love not only *restored* her marriage but *transformed* my father's life and *protected* mine as well.

Chapter 6: Why Is It Important To Forgive Immediately?

The Power of Immediate Forgiveness.

It may take a season to arrive at the place you *desire* in your heart; however, you will get there. If you did not expect a change in your life, you would not be reading this book with the hope it will help you. That says a lot about who you are as a person.

Your hurt may be *deep*. You may not understand *why* you hurt, *how* you were hurt or why it is so *hard* to forgive the person who hurt you. However, the wall you are facing *will* come down.

Once someone asks you to forgive them, it is vital to *immediately* release forgiveness to heal the relationship. Also, if you are married, it will help you both to move *past* the hurt.

Immediately means without an interval of time: STRAIGHTWAY – I will make that call immediately.

You probably think immediately is a *strong* word when it comes to forgiving someone. Stick with me. You will understand as we move forward.

Forgiveness is a *process*.

I hope that this chapter will help you *start* the process because people think differently about forgiving. For example, some individuals may think they had every *right* to do what they did to you, yet you got hurt due to what they did.

They may ask you to forgive them because of hurtful words you feel you cannot recover from. You have a right to *feel* the way you are feeling, but you do not have a right to *stay* in that dilemma. The *quicker* you forgive, the *better* it will be for your wellbeing.

"Or despisest thou the riches of His goodness and forbearance and longsuffering; not knowing that the goodness of God leadeth thee to repentance?"(Roman 2:4).

Use The Instrument of Healing

The Goodness and Kindness of God in your heart are an *instrument* of healing that will minister to each of you. For example, if you are married to an unbeliever, they will *see* how the Power of God is working in your life, and it will be a *testimony* that may change their life.

Have you reached a point in your life where you are at your wit's end, and you do not know what to do?

Trust God!

This book is a message of Hope. Forgiving someone is a part of that Hope, giving you both an opportunity to *recover* and *grow* from what happened.

Remember The Lost Soul

God's Word provides an answer to the question of what happens when you make yourself *available* to be used by Him to *save* a *lost* soul. The verse below is self-explanatory on what the Lord will do *through* you to *reach* your loved one.

"For the unbelieving husband is sanctified by the wife, and the unbelieving wife is sanctified by the husband: else were your children unclean; but now are they holy," (1 Corinthians 7:14).

When someone *asks* you to forgive them, it not only releases *them* but *you* as well. That is why it is important never to *hold back* from forgiving someone.

You may feel *justified* to hold back because you want them to *keep* hurting and *remain* reminded of what they did to you. Your behavior may appear appropriate until you hold it up against God's Word.

Your reaction is *self-righteousness*, feeling they deserve to feel remorse until you decide you are *ready* to forgive them. Remember, *two* wrongs do not make a *right*.

Forgiving someone who hurt you is both for their benefit and yours, so you all can experience the *healing* process and *restoration* in the relationship. When someone is *asking* for your forgiveness, a lot is involved. Rebuilding *trust* is one of them.

Rebuilding can be highly challenging if the *repeat* offender makes the *same* promises repeatedly yet *never* changes.

The question now is, how do you move from *where* you are to a *better* place that will give each of you *hope* that things will change for the best?

Seek The Right Help

The following scripture is one of my favorites.

"My people are destroyed for lack of knowledge: because thou hast rejected knowledge, I will also reject thee, that thou shalt be no priest to Me: seeing thou hast forgotten the law of thy God, I will also forget thy children," (Hosea 4:6).

A *lack* of knowledge will *affect* a believer and an unbeliever *alike*. The only way you can *gain* an understanding of what you are facing is to *ask* questions. You are not *alone* in what you are going through. But, unfortunately, the enemy of your soul wants you to think you are the *only* person going through it, and that is far from the truth.

The question you need to ask yourself is why you are not seeking the *right* help. It may be because the human part of you wants everyone to *agree* with you and *affirm* you to do what you *want* to do. But, unfortunately, that is giving up because all you are looking for is *justification* for your mistakes.

Are You In An Abusive Relationship?

If you are in a domestic violence situation, it is best to get *out* before getting hurt *beyond* recovery. Find a place where you can think *clearly*. It is not the will of God for your life to be in harm's way.

If you are not a victim of domestic violence and *see* hope for your marriage, do not give up. Do not turn your back on the future of your marriage, even if a *wedge* has come between the both of you.

God is very clear about prayer and what can *hinder* your prayer life. God's Word cautions the believing husband. He must forgive *immediately* so the answers to his prayers will not be delayed.

While pastoring in a troubled marriage, I kept this verse before me because I did not want my prayers to be hindered as a pastor or husband.

"Likewise, ye husbands, dwell with them according to knowledge, giving honour unto the wife, as unto the weaker vessel, and as being heirs together of the grace of life; that your prayers be not hindered," (1 Peter 3:7).

God's Word is *true,* and there is no way to get *around* it. Therefore, you must operate *within* God's guidelines to have your prayers answered.

Fight The Good Fight of Faith

Looking back, you should say you made *every* effort to win. God's Word instructs you to fight the *good* fight in faith. Without faith, it is *impossible* to please God.

"But without faith it is impossible to please Him: for he that cometh to God must believe that He is, and that He is a Rewarder of them that diligently seek Him," (Hebrews 11:6).

Make every effort to fight *right*. No one wins in a bad fight. However, a *good* battle is life-changing, and you will *learn* something about yourself to make your life *better*.

Things may seem *muddy* right now. You may be *slipping* and *sliding* through life, unable to find a *stable* place to hold on to. But, your help is on the way. God has not *forgotten* you. He will provide a way out with *peace* of mind.

"There hath no temptation taken you but such as is common to man: but God is faithful, Who will not suffer you to be tempted above that ye are able; but will with the temptation also make a way to escape, that ye may be able to bear it," (1 Corinthians 10:13).

Your Help Is On The Way

Like the Apostle Paul, you want to say you *fought* the good fight and *kept* the faith. Therefore, do not walk away because the *good* fight for your marriage will be *beneficial* in the long run.

My first wife always asked me, "Why do you always bring God up every time we talk about our marriage?"

I replied, "That is the only way we are going to make it." Needless to say, we did not.

I hope this verse encourages you to keep *standing* and *trusting* God, so at the end of it all, you know you made *every* effort to bring glory to Him in saving your marriage.

"I have fought a good fight, I have finished my course, I have kept the faith," (2 Timothy 2:4).

Sometimes, life is like playing baseball. The baseball diamond is your family circle. You are on *second* base trying to make it *home*. Make sure you have *covered* your bases, even though you may be *struggling* to know God's will.

5 Steps To Making It Home And Trusting God With Your Heart

Step One: Make it *known* you want to *save* your marriage and make every *effort* to change and do your part.

Step Two: Know *where* you are standing in the relationship, whether on second or third base because you know you have not yet made a home run.

A home run means you are in a *safe* place. However, until you make an effort to find out *where* you stand, you will not know where to *start* your efforts to help *restore* your marriage.

Step Three: Gather *resources* and help from the right individuals because you want to know what you *need* and where you stand in your marriage.

Step Four: Ask God to bless you with a *prayer partner* you can be *accountable* to and know will *walk* with you in this season and keep your hope *alive*.

Step Five: Read God's Word until your cup *overflows* with change, faith, fortitude, and strength; that only God can give you for the journey you are both on.

Taking these steps with determination, passion, and a prayerful, forgiving heart will *lift* the burden. Your swiftness to pardon will *remove* the extra load of unforgiveness *blocking* the way.

If you both *agree*, you will see *progress*. If you both *trust* God's faithfulness, you will have a marriage that will bless *others* and give the next couple hope that they too can make it through their struggles.

Agreement is a *powerful* tool that will help you along the way. "Can two walk together, except they be agreed?" (Amos 3:3).

"Verily I say unto you, Whatsoever ye shall bind on earth shall be bound in heaven: and whatsoever ye shall loose on earth shall be loosed in heaven. Again I say unto you, That if two of you shall agree on earth as touching any thing that they shall ask, it shall be done for them of My Father Which is in heaven," (Matthew 18:18-19).

Chapter 7: Holding On To Hurt Until Tomorrow

Tomorrow Is Not Promised.

Your Tomorrow will be the *same* as your Today if you *continue* holding on to hurt. The purpose of this chapter is to *challenge* you to deal with what you have been *unwilling* to face.

Life is not easy, even when with faith in God. You will face challenges *every* day. It is time to be honest and straightforward about the hurt you are going through that has neither been *addressed* nor *resolved*.

When the 9/11 Terrorist Attack happened, I worked for Orkin Pest Control in the New Orleans area. I was living on the military base with my wife. I was in my *second* marriage. While pumping gas, a soldier asked me if I heard what had just happened in New York regarding the planes flying into the Twin Towers.

My very first thought was to wonder if my wife was *safe* because she was in New

York at the time on assignment. So many thoughts were racing through my mind. Since flights were grounded, how would she get back home? What would I say to our sons once they arrived home from school?

Thankfully, she was *unharmed*. The military made sure everyone got home safely. I met her on the plane. I was carrying a dozen roses to *welcome* her home. But, instead, she hid and ran out behind someone as if our relationship did not matter. That was one of *many* red flags in my marriage.

In prayer, I fell on my face and asked God to help me get past the hurt. In my first book, *Forgive Who? How A Man Can Forgive His Ex-Wife And Move On With Life*, I share how important it is to forgive *immediately* so that the pain will not *control* your life. Forgiving *quickly* was not easy for me to do.

The Lord Will See You Through

You may be experiencing a different level of hurt and pain. My personal testimony is my relationship with The Lord got me *through* those challenging moments when I felt *less* than a man.

I had many moments like that in different situations during my *failing* marriage. My wife was going through pain and attempting to *build* a marriage life and future with a husband she did not love. How she did that, only God knows. But, I *applaud* her for standing strong while perhaps hoping her heart would *change* toward me.

After the ripples from the 9/11 tragedy settled, I remember driving down many streets, reading signs in yards *inviting* everyone to *pray* for America. What was interesting about that time and season was so many people were praying and going to church, *looking* for answers.

That was an excellent opportunity for the church to *rise* to the occasion and *minister* to the hurting. But, unfortunately, as fast as the hurting *filled* the pews, so they *left* because they did not get the answers they were *desperately* searching for.

Today, many are looking for answers to *solve* their marital problems and know *why* their lives are so full of hurt and frustration. They wonder why they cannot seem to move forward in life, *past* the discomfort and pain.

Your Marriage Has An Enemy

You may be wondering how you can compare 9/11 to *hurting* marriages and *broken* lives. Well, I am glad you asked. We have an enemy in *strategic* places who desires for our love for each other to grow *cold*, for there to be no *answer* to failing marriages, that *none* would be saved.

I am called as a watchman, *standing* on the wall and *shouting* as loud as I can, that we have the *answer* to failing marriages in God's Word. The Word of God can *heal* and *keep* your marriage together.

You are reading this book because you are *looking* for answers. You may *hurt* in your heart. You may wonder how I can help you. After going through divorce *twice*, how can I be an excellent example of faith and fortitude?

That is the very reason I can.

Why My Marriage Failed

Holding onto hurt does not *help* you or anyone else. Anyone who holds on to their pain does so because of their *will*, pride, and *refusal* to trust God. God will come through if you find a place of *agreement* with your mate, and you both *trust* Him.

The Lord would have come through for my wife and me if we had *agreed*, *invited* the Lord in, and *asked* for His help. The Lord did not *fail* us. Instead, we failed God by not trusting Him to *keep* His Word.

God keeps His Word. He will walk with you both through this challenging time. But, when it comes down to it, my wife and I failed each other.

Walking away and not being willing to solve your problems will backfire on you both, causing *more* problems. Do not *wait* until Tomorrow. Instead, start Today, this very moment. This time, *invite* the Lord in to help you. If you are not a believer, I share the Plan of Salvation with you at the end of this book. The Plan of Salvation is God's blueprint for you.

To the believer who has decided to throw in the towel, please *reconsider* and *trust* God to do what you could not do. You will never be able to do it on your own. Please read the verse below for *Hope* and *Strength*. Handle your business Today with God's help.

"Take therefore no thought for the morrow: for the morrow shall take thought for the things of itself. Sufficient unto the day is the evil thereof," (Matthew 6:34).

God Is Your Accessible Help

Whatever you are facing today in your marriage, know that God is a very *Present* Help. God will *help* you and *carry* you both through it if you would only line up your will with His will.

"God is our Refuge and Strength, a very Present Help in trouble," (Psalm 46:1).

We all have had enemies. They come in many forms. If you want someone to agree with you even when you are wrong, that is a telltale sign you are talking to the *wrong* person. It is time to make some changes *before* it is too late; before you get so far out, you can *never* recover because your will is *fighting* The Lord's will for your life.

Never is a *long* time. Not knowing God's very *best* for you will affect your future decisions. If you do not *awaken* to what you need to do, you will continue to *loop* through life in *failing* relationships.

You cannot give God your *full* attention until your will becomes His will. So on the days you feel like giving up, you need to *rely* on God to help you stay *strong* and not give up, especially on yourself. You are important, and so is the *destiny* of your marriage.

Do Not Believe The Enemy's Lies

When you are in the same storm over and over again, the enemy will try to make you think *nothing* will change. That is not true. If you look for the correct *solutions* to what you are facing, you will know that things can *change* if you are *willing* to put the work in and not give up.

When we as a nation finally got past the 9/11 tragedy, those who caused the pain were caught, punished, and the cell group that was planning to bring further harm was discovered and exposed.

Would you believe there may be *someone* in your life who does not want you to make it? Guess what? That could very well be *you*. Perhaps, you are *prone* to self-sabotage, and you give up too *quickly*.

You can *cause* your pain by not being willing to face what you are going through. You *convince* yourself you do not need to change, and you can handle it all by yourself. That is why Tomorrow will never come unless you are *willing* to face the music.

Face The Music

Read your Bible and *know* that God's Word will *answer* you and *help* you in all you are facing. Read the verse below and *recognize* God's promise to you.

"And we know that all things work together for good to them that love God, to them who are the called according to His purpose," (Roman 8:28).

You are not living if you are holding on to hurt. If in some way you have *smothered* the pain through drinking, drugs, or work, every time you look in the mirror, you will *remember* why you did what you did, trying to *forget* the hurt, but to no avail, because the wound is still there.

This book is about *helping* you and *directing* you to the help you need. At the back of the book, I provide information to get you started locating the help you need for your marriage and relationships with others.

You Affect People Around You

Your marriage affects *everyone* around you. There is no way to get around it. You may have heard, "Leave your family problems at home and your career problems at work."

You are *human*. You can only take so much until you *cannot* take any more. So facing your problems without God is a challenge.

You can take some steps by putting down names of individuals you know will walk with you during this dark time and speak the *truth* in your life. Seek those willing to address the *tough* questions without *compromising* your destiny. Identify who will help you face Tomorrow by dealing with your hurt Today.

Put a *strategy* together through prayer and make sure you have the right circle of friends. Finally, realize you will never find peace in *ignoring* or *covering up* the pain until Tomorrow.

God loves you and will help you if you *call* upon Him in times of *trouble* and even in the good times. It is all about *relationships*, and how much the Lord *loves* you and *cares* for you. Do not allow the enemy to make you think it is not worth it.

Let these words *encourage* you. "For I know the thoughts that I think toward you, saith the Lord, thoughts of peace, and not of evil, to give you an expected end," (Jeremiah 29:11).

It is not the will of God for someone to beat up on you and cause *harm* to your life. If you have children, I encourage you to pack up this book and some clothes and get out *now* because domestic violence is an epidemic in America. God's Word is very clear about how we should live with each other and how a man should *love* his wife.

"If it be possible, as much as lieth in you, live peaceably with all men," (Romans 12: 18).

"Husbands, love your wives, even as Christ also loved the church, and gave Himself for it," (Ephesians 5:25).

There Is No Hurt Too Deep For His Love

Your hurt may be *deep*. Know that God's Love can go deep and *heal* your marriage if you are both willing to put the work in for a change.

When it comes to domestic violence, I will encourage you to seek professional help before doing it yourself. Know that it is not

God's will for anyone to become a *victim* because someone *chooses* to allow evil to remain in their heart.

God's Love can reach the impossible if you are *willing* to allow Him in. Conversely, some individuals use Christianity without a heart change to *deceive* many. If you are not in tune with God and your life is in shambles, you need *help* to make the right decisions, especially when it comes to domestic violence.

Remember, Tomorrow is not promised to anyone. But, with God's help and the right individuals in your life, you can *start* on the road to change. It was never God's plan for you to carry hurt in your heart because hurt only causes *more* hurt when you do not *resolve* it.

Chapter 8: Do You Need A Divorce To Find The Right One?

I Have Been Through Divorce Twice!

I can remember the hurt, sadness, and pain I experienced during my *second* divorce. I began to look for help so history would not repeat itself if a *third* marriage were in my future. Divorce Care was my *lifeline* of support. I went through the thirteen-week course *twice*, then became a volunteer for *three* more sessions to help and encourage others, for a total of *five* times.

I heard a popular TV host make a statement about *why* he divorced. He said that you need to divorce someone to find the *right* one. So I knew this was a subject I needed to address in my new book, *Please Help Me Save My Marriage!*

This celebrity has the *ear* of America.

He stated that to *find* happiness, you need to *divorce* the one you are with now. So he divorced his wife to find the *right* one, the one he is with now. Since he has *professed* to believe in Jesus Christ, I waited to see if he would say that The Lord could help *heal* a broken marriage if both individuals would seek Him.

If you *truly* know God, use your platform to spread the *truth* that helps others when they ask questions instead of applying worldly philosophies.

You are probably thinking, "Donald, you have had two divorces. How can you help me?"

I can help you by *admitting* my failures with the hopes you can *learn* from what I *did not* do and what I *needed* to do. Your marriage can only work if you both agree that you *want* the marriage saved. Together, you must decide to *listen* and *learn* from people who can genuinely help you both.

A Lesson From Seminary School

While in seminary, pursuing my Master's Degree in Theology, I took a counseling course. My professor taught us that we could only work with the *percentage* that a person is *willing* to give. If they only provide a *low* percentage, you can work with that *until* they are eager to share more.

That may be where you are now because *all* your hope is gone. Do not give up. God can take the *little* you are willing to give and *increase* it if you have *faith* and *trust* in His Grace and Mercy.

Even with a low percentage of strength, the verse below clearly states what The Lord is eager to do on your behalf if you trust Him.

"And we know that all things work together for good to them that love God, to them who are the called according to His purpose," (Romans 8:28).

Do Not Throw Your Marriage Away!

Do not give up on your marriage because you have not seen your spouse *become* the person you *expected*. If you are in a *questionable* relationship that *feels* right, but the person you are with is *still* married to someone else, you need to step back and ask God to help you move on.

You are engaging in a relationship that is not legitimate, even if your flesh may be telling you it is alright. Deep down, you know your heart is *unsettled* because God's commandments about being with someone who is still married to another are very clear.

Remember, they are *still* married.

You should *never* date a married person. The enemy has a plan to *trap* you, and if you are not prayerful, you will *sabotage* your future following what *you* want rather than what God desires for you.

Entertaining someone on the side while you are married will *muddy* the water, and you will not hear from God clearly because you are in *blatant* sin and disobedience. God is not going to confirm His will for your life while you are living in *rebellion* to His standards.

The verse below gives God's mind on what it takes to see His will in your life. "If ye be willing and obedient, ye shall eat the good of the land," (Isaiah 1:19).

Are You Willing And Obedient?

God knows what is *best* for you. If you are *willing* to obey His Voice and Word, then the outcome will be beneficial in the long run.

I was not surprised when the celebrity made the statement about divorce because he has written a book endorsing couples becoming *intimate* 90 days into their relationship, even though they are not married.

"This know also, that in the last days perilous times shall come. For men shall be lovers of their own selves, covetous, boasters, proud, blasphemers, disobedient to parents, unthankful, unholy...Having a form of godliness, but denying the power thereof: from such turn away," (2 Timothy 3:1-2,5).

God's Word does not permit intimacy *before* marriage. Take God at His Word and His plan for your life. If you are honest, the *trouble* you are in now is because of *your disobedience.*

"Flee fornication. Every sin that a man doeth is without the body; but he that committeth fornication sinneth against his own body. What? know ye not that your body is the temple of the Holy Ghost which is in you, which ye have of God, and ye are not your own? For ye are bought with a price: therefore glorify God in your body, and in your spirit, which are God's," (1 Corinthians 6:18-20).

If you are in an *abusive* marriage and your husband is beating upon you, then you need to get out *now* and seek professional help because you do not want to be hurt beyond what you can heal from.

Easy Is Not Always Right

Divorcing someone to find the right one is not the answer. It is *tempting* and easy to choose this option, especially if you are the *only* one that wants things to work out.

Put your thinking cap on. How can you *trust* a person in marriage if they *left* someone to be with you? There is a good chance they will do it to you when the going gets tough in your relationship or when someone else comes along saying what they want to hear.

I pastored for over a decade while my second marriage was in trouble. My wife made it clear that counseling was not an option for us. What you can *learn* from my failures is not to *ignore* the signs in the beginning. Try your best to get help *early* on, and maybe then you can *save* your marriage before it is too late.

I am determined to help others with this message of Hope because so much is involved when you go through a divorce, especially when children are affected or get caught in the middle.

The Easy Way Out! Really?

Divorce has been called the *easy* way to happiness and contentment. However, divorcing someone to find the right one is not your way out. If you are a believer and know Christ as your Savior, He has a *better* plan. He will help you and give you *peace* that passes all understanding.

"And the peace of God, which passeth all understanding, shall keep your hearts and minds through Christ Jesus," (Philippians 4:7).

You may be in a period of confusion. You must regain your footing and get a *clear* direction of what is next. Your decision is about *your* life, the ones you *love*, and your *future*.

The Gift Nobody Wants

I know all too well the pain of divorce and the thoughts that *attack* your mind. It can be stressful and painful. Pain is a *gift* nobody wants. Pain is an *indicator* that something is wrong, and you need to give your attention to what is *causing* the pain. If it is an individual *outside* your marriage, this brings even more pain.

Surround yourself with people that will *keep* you in prayer and encourage you, who will *always* tell you the truth and not *compromise* God's Word when giving counsel during this stressful time. I look back now, and I am thankful I had the right individuals in my corner, *praying* for me and *encouraging* me to stand firm.

Divorcing someone to find the right person is not the answer, especially if your spouse is *willing* to work things out with you. I read a statement that millennials are doing life *their* way and not the traditional way to *save* their marriage. Taking matters into your hands and *excluding* God is a huge mistake.

Divorce Is Not The Answer

If you are *willing* to put in the work to save the marriage, that is *better* than divorce. You both will be blessed *beyond* where you are now. If someone other than your spouse is telling you they are the one for you; there are several indicators for you to know they are not God's will for your life.

You cannot honestly and scripturally *pray* they replace your wife. You cannot get wise *counsel* from God's Word approving them. Your Pastor will not *endorse* them.

My prayer for you is that you will make the right decisions and not live with regret. I have added resources at the back of the book to help you along the way and show you how serious I am about helping in any way I can.

Here is my direct email address: donaldsmithtx@gmail.com

Chapter 9: Pain Is A Gift Nobody Wants

Gifts Often Bring Joy.

When you think of a gift, it makes you *smile,* especially if you are on the *receiving* end. I love receiving gifts. My sister is the one person I know who loves to *give* gifts and make others happy.

This chapter will deal with the *negative* end of receiving a gift through the pain you are going through. The gift is *hidden* in what you can *learn* from it. Appreciate the lesson, even if you brought it on yourself through your disobedience.

Maybe you *sabotaged* your effort to get ahead in life because you of someone's faulty advice and counsel that you followed. Perhaps you are like David, who had a friend he used to eat with turn *against* him.

"Yea, mine own familiar friend, in whom I trusted, which did eat of my bread, hath lifted up his heel against me," (Psalm 41:9).

Pain comes in *different* forms. Pain could even come through a sickness that puts a *strain* on your marriage relationship.

One of the *first* things you may be *tempted* to do when pain arrives unwelcomed is to *blame* someone else. Of course, you could be *accurate* in your assessment of what is happening to you. However, I want you to look at pain as a *gift* because when pain *tangibly* happens to you, it has your *attention*.

Examine the pain you are going through in your marriage or as a single person who *wants* to be married. Learn the lesson the pain is trying to *teach* you because life has a way of *repeating* itself if you missed the learning opportunity.

Avoiding Pain Will Not Fix Your Problems

You and another imperfect human being may face *failure* in life and *experience* pain. How you deal with it *together* will determine the outcome. This is crucial because you can make a *wrong* turn if you are not *prayerful* and *discerning* God's will for your next step.

Making a bad turn because you received counsel from the *wrong* person will hurt *both* of you. When you are in pain, you do not do your *best* thinking. You are *aching,* and you want a *quick* remedy, even if it means *divorce.* Yet, that option does not *resolve* your marital problems.

Many married couples have chosen to go through the pain of *staying* together, thinking there is no answer to the problems they are facing. They are not happy. They no longer *enjoy* being with each other. So, they go through the *motions* of marriage. That was never God's plan for marriage because His Word says, "It is not good for man to be alone."

You Do Not Have To Feel Alone

It was never God's intention for us to be *married,* only to feel *alone.* "And the Lord God said, It is not good that the man should be alone; I will make him an help meet for him," (Genesis 2:18).

Let us examine the *elements* of this verse:

A. And the Lord said

B. It is not good that man should be *alone*

C. God recognized the *need* in Adam's life

D. Adam needs *help* to meet life challenges

E. God's *Word*

F. A *helper*

G. A *wife*

A *suitable* woman was the answer. Her name was Eve. It is fitting that a man who is alone *receives* a help-mate. A *third* person potentially *harms* the relationship and marriage. The enemy does not want us to be a helpful *resource* for each other.

A man needs to listen to The Holy Spirit and his wife. It is of paramount importance to *study* God's Word daily. Keep in mind; help is what you need when you have done *all* you know to do.

Reach Out To Your Pastor For Guidance

If you do not have a pastor, there is information at the end of the book to help you get the assistance you need. The last thing I want is to write a book and leave you without *additional* resources to utilize *after* you have followed the instructions, suggestions, and directions I share.

My second marriage started with God as the focus. But, unfortunately, something happened along the way. I hope you can *learn* from my failure to *keep* my marriage together. Everything I am *sharing* with you is what I learned from my failures and what I should have done *instead*.

Have you ever looked back over your life and *wished* you had done something differently? Maybe you should have *listened* to rebuke and correction. By *refusing* to listen, I created *more* hurt on top of the pain. I regret I did not listen to godly counsel in the beginning. However, God did send *many* godly voices to try and help me get back on track.

The two verses below reminded me of God's provision and a *warning* of what would happen if I did not listen and obey. But, unfortunately, this is what has happened in many marriages.

"Thy word is a lamp unto my feet, and a light unto my path," (Psalm 119: 105).

"Pride goeth before destruction, and an haughty spirit before a fall," (Proverbs 16:18).

Many of us married *again* too soon and still *feel* the pain of the Past. That is why I wrote my first book, *Forgive Who? How A Man Can Forgive His Ex-Wife And Move On With Life*, a book for men and the women who love them, to help both of them get past the failures of Yesterday.

The Buck Stops With You

It is time to take *responsibility* where you failed. Be honest, and try not to point fingers like Adam and Eve. Do not *blame* each other or the devil.

Take responsibility where *you* failed.

How many fingers does it take to blame someone? *Only one!* The other four are pointing back at *you.*

How you *handle* pain will determine the *outcome* for everyone involved. I know pain *hurts* significantly when you have not *healed* from it.

Pain Is A Wake-Up Call

If you do not give it the *attention* it requires, your marriage may be headed to Divorce Court. But, that does not need to happen. At a court hearing, the judge walks in. Everyone stands up to honor the Justice of the Peace. Finally, with the banging of the gavel, a significant chapter of your life is *over* in an instant.

Don't you think it is time to take a stand and *fix* what is broken in your life and marriage? Stop *allowing* the enemy to make you think your life will never get better.

Do not allow a court to *decide* for you.

You can *save* your marriage by the Grace of God. The Lord is *willing* to help you both if you would only *ask* Him.

Become A Listener

Remember Pontius Pilate's wife? She *warned* Pilate, but because of *pride*, he did not listen. Pilate *rejected* her counsel, and we know what happened as a result. If a man is honest, he can think back to times he should have listened.

I can remember a time we were looking for a building for our ministries to meet in. The Lord spoke to my former wife about the location. I am glad I *listened*. We ended up using that property for over four years. We even *supported* a Bible college that needed a home. We did not charge them any rent or fee, which was a blessing.

It is no fun going through pain, being *unable* to talk with your significant other, and never *benefiting* from their influence and wisdom. The pain will shut down your progress.

Remember, God says, it is not good for man to be *alone*. He has *given* you everything you need in each other. With His guidance, you can have victory.

A man's wife should be able to take him from good to *great*. "She will do him good and not evil all the days of her life," (Proverbs 31:12).

Chapter 10: Why Do You Keep Experiencing The Same Seasons?

Seasons Come And Go.

Some seasons stick around longer than others or seem to *repeat* themselves. That is what is addressed in this chapter. Why do you keep seeing the same *recurring* event in your life, whether you are a believer or non-believer?

God's Word states that the sun shines on the just and unjust. "That ye may be the children of your Father Which is in heaven: for He maketh His sun to rise on the evil and on the good, and sendeth rain on the just and on the unjust," (Matthew 5:45).

Have you ever stopped to consider *why* you keep *experiencing* the same things over and over again? Maybe it is time to consider what is *influencing* your decision each day. Why do you find yourself back at the *same* place? Why does it seem you cannot get *out* of the twilight zone.

The *correct* answer will help you make a decision that will cause your results and seasons to *change*. Only then will you *stop* seeing the same things recurring in your life. When it happens *repetitively*, it affects your marriage and the entire family.

You may have said what many others have, "Here I go again." When you get *tired* of hitting the brick wall, you will *wake* up to what is happening. You are now *ready* to make the necessary *changes*.

The Law of Displacement

Once you *decide* that things will change in your life and you are *willing* to do what is needed, please keep in mind that whatever you discard needs to be *replaced* with better.

As a believer, you understand where I am going with this. "When the unclean spirit is gone out of a man, he walketh through dry places seeking rest; and finding none, he saith, I will return unto my house whence I came out," (Luke 11:24).

You have an enemy. His goal is to keep you heading in the same *miserable* direction; unending *unhappiness* and *discouragement.*

Luke 11:24 is a statement of *ownership,* revealing what the evil spirit would do to be restored.

The unclean spirit said, "I will return unto my house whence I came out." The unclean spirit has laid *claim* to the house from which he was evicted. The unclean spirit speaks with *confidence* that returning is the *only* option.

The Scripture states the spirit walked through *dry* places seeking *rest*. Rest, to the unclean spirit, is causing unrest in *your* life, causing you to go through the *same* things over and over again.

It is the will of God for you to be *free* and *clean* in spirit, soul, and body. You cannot *hear* God clearly if your heart stays in a state of turmoil.

Change How You Start Your Day

Over the years, I have heard this statement about getting up on the *wrong* side of the bed. "One day, I feel like a nut, and some days I do not. Who I am today for sure depends on how I get up in the morning. So I will decide on who I am that day."

My suggestion would be to go *back* to bed for five minutes and then get up on the *right* side of the bed. God has blessed you to see another day that was not promised. It is time to get up with *praise, gratitude,* and *thankfulness* in your heart so that God will bless your efforts and others in the process.

If you do not know Jesus Christ as your *personal* Savior, you are doing life *alone.* You have an enemy that is keeping you from *knowing* Christ and how much He *loves* you. Jesus desires to bless your life and give you the answers you need to confront what you are facing in your marriage.

You can *recover* with the Lord's help.

The Lord Is Your Defense

Remember, the unclean spirit *threatened* to return because it was not happy with its present condition. When it returns, it finds the house *clean.*

"And when he cometh, he findeth it swept and garnished. Then goeth he, and taketh to him seven other spirits more wicked than himself, and they enter in, and dwell there: and the last state of that man is worse than the first," (Luke 11:25-26).

Earlier I stated that once you *discard* something from your life, it needs to be *replaced.* It needs to be replaced with God's life-giving Power. If you do not *allow* God to restore you and make you whole again, that unclean spirit will return with *vigor* and a stronger voice because it brings *other* foul spirits with it, causing your present state to be *worse* than before.

An unclean spirit is a demon who wants *multiple* demons *to control* your life. An unclean spirit is after one thing, for you to make decisions without asking God and move toward a destructive outcome before waiting on His answer. That unclean spirit's goal is for you to end up making decisions and *doing* things you said you would *never* do. The *wicked* voices from these unclean spirits seek to keep you going from one relationship to another and sleeping around with different individuals.

It is sad to say, many believers think it is *acceptable* to God for them to have sex *outside* of marriage. Get your testimony back. Be an effective *witness* with a life that brings glory to God. The Body of Christ needs *strong* unions that have gone through the storms of life with a testimony of *victory*.

What Bible Are You Reading?

I am not sure what Bible is being read by those who think it is *acceptable* to have sex *outside* marriage. You need to be very prayerful because your spiritual condition will be affected if you are not building up your faith in God's Word.

To avoid reading the *wrong* material for helping your marriage, you need a good Bible. If you are studying the New

International Version (NIV) Bible, keep in mind many important verses are *missing* from that particular version of The Bible. I *strongly* suggest the King James Version (KJV) of The Bible.

Keep in your mind and heart that The Lord wants to be the most *dominant* Voice in your life. He wants you to have *answers* regarding why you keep *repeating* your *sad* seasons. So many marriages are going through the same cycle, and that can be discouraging.

If you have been married *several* times but have never forgiven your former spouses, that can affect your present state as well. You begin to wonder why you are going through so many divorces and remarriages and cannot seem to get it right.

If you are married now and consider divorce the *only* answer to your problem, please step back and pray. If you are *enduring* physical abuse, you need to get out before you are hurt beyond recovery. But, unfortunately, the enemy is unrelenting in keeping you in *confusion*.

Walk Away From Confusion

Remember, God is not the Author of confusion. "For God is not the Author of confusion, but of peace, as in all churches of the saints," (1 Corinthians 14:33).

Who have you been listening to, and what *results* are you seeing? The person you are talking to about your marriage may not have a prayer life. They may know *nothing* about God or how to counsel you with *godly* advice.

Think about this. If everyone *agrees* with you because you want them in your corner and they tell you what you *want* to hear because they are your BFF, they will not *challenge* you or tell you the truth. They will not *drive* you to trust God and pray. Have they helped you to do God's will and save your marriage?

Encourage Yourself In The Lord

God *loves* you and desires that you build up your faith. God gives a *clear* picture of how you should encourage yourself and stay *focused* on Him. Hopefully, if you are an unbeliever, you will decide to *accept* Christ in your heart and life by the end of this book.

"Redeeming the time, because the days are evil. Wherefore be ye not unwise, but understanding what the will of the Lord is. And be not drunk with wine, wherein is excess; but be filled with the Spirit; Speaking to yourselves in psalms and hymns and spiritual songs, singing and making melody in your heart to the Lord," (Ephesians 5:16-19).

You must speak to yourself in such a way that it *builds* you up. Know the will of God. Have you ever confessed bad things about yourself, put yourself down and come to the conclusion that your marriage is over? The enemy always wants you to think the *worst* of yourself. If you take on that belief, you will fall out of agreement with what the Lord says about you.

You may be wondering how you can learn *anything* from someone who has been through two divorces. First, you can learn from my failures and mistakes. Second, you can *fight* another day with prayer. Finally, you can *receive* godly advice that will help save your marriage.

Do Not Step Out of The Will of God

If I had fought the good fight of faith *early* on in my first marriage, we would have never divorced. Instead, I listened to my counsel. I wanted to move on and begin a new relationship. But, unfortunately, I was *out* of the will of God. The lady I saw at the time was never in God's plan for my life.

Even though it had been two years since my first wife and I parted ways, and we were going through the process of divorce, I had not healed. I look back now and realize the mistake I made.

I announced to everyone I was in the will of God, and this woman I was seeing was the one. My first wife and I were not yet *officially* divorced. Yes, our papers were filed, but in God's sight, we were *still* married.

How could I be praying about being with someone else while I was not a *free* man? Yet, I had Scripture references validating my moving on with life, *or so I thought.*

Have You Heard From God?

Today, I am a *cautious* yet prayerful man. I am *careful* to say what God's plan will be concerning marriage again in my life. I realize I made a *significant* mistake, and I paid for it by going through a *second* divorce. I believed I had heard from the Lord concerning my second marriage, but I found out later I was in error.

At the time, I was *convinced* to the core I was in the will of God. But, as time moved on, I knew something was *wrong.* It seemed like I could not see the light at the end of the tunnel. The day she asked me for a divorce, she admitted *regretting* the first day she married me.

Right then, all the red flags I saw over our years of marriage made sense. My second wife *never* loved me. She was not married to me in *spirit*, but in name only. I mention a little more about this in my book, *Forgive Who? How A Man Can Forgive His Ex-Wife And Move On With Life*.

Admit *where* you went wrong and *stop* the cycle of pain. God can and *will* heal a broken heart. It is not God's will for you to *continue* enduring the same *miserable* season. Your marriage can be rescued if you are willing to put the work in.

Are You Committed?

You automatically decide to be married in *name* only when you fail to give your *whole* heart to the *survival* of your marriage. Your confession must line up with The Word of God. You must come in *agreement* with what the Lord says about you and your marriage.

The verse below is very clear about the desire and the will of God to *speak* to you.

"My sheep hear My voice, and I know them, and they follow Me," (John 10:27).

Do not be blind to why you keep undergoing the same seasons in life. Bad decisions will keep you trapped in the same *disappointing* cycle of events. That is why you end up thinking your *only* option is divorce. It is not the will of God for you to go through the same *upsetting* things repeatedly. Instead, God desires that you *learn* and *grow* in the direction of His will for your life.

Be *honest* with yourself. Get the answers you need so you can know *why* things seem to always take a turn for the *worst*, and history keeps repeating itself.

Shun Ulterior Motives

A while back, a lady who was having problems in her marriage reached out to me. She had a question. I thought this was going to be an opportunity to see the *fruit* of my labor. But, unfortunately, the situation went south as soon as she opened her mouth because of her mindset and spirit.

She stated that she had married *out* of the will of God because her husband was not what she had prayed for, so she was filing for a divorce. She pointedly said to me, "You never know what God is doing."

I shared with her that God *hates* divorce. If her husband agreed, they should get some marital counseling. She had *ulterior* motives that she wanted me to participate in. She kept saying she did not want to run me away, but like Joseph, I ran! I did not leave my coat behind though.

Thank God for phone counseling!

The change will not come if you choose not to deal with what is in your heart. You end up *repeating* history over and over again. Your decisions will be based on *past* hurts and failures. You will continue *blaming* others. Like Adam and Eve, there is a *tendency* to blame others.

Hearing God's Voice

I decided to save the *best* of this chapter for last. How *sweet* it is to *hear* God's Voice and know His will for your life and marriage. Hearing His loving Voice will bring *comfort* to your life and marriage. Delighting yourself in The Lord will always be *advantageous.*

"Delight thyself also in the Lord: and He shall give thee the desires of thine heart," (Psalm 37:4).

For you to *know* God's will, you must *develop* a relationship with Him. If you are an unbeliever and have not accepted The Lord into your heart, be sure to read the information at the back of the book on how to do so. I also include suggestions on how to *find* a good church where you can *grow* in your faith.

Delighting yourself in the Lord is the *key* to hearing His Voice. It means you will have a *desire* to do God's will and to *please* Him. I am guilty of standing in the pulpit *testifying* that it was God's will for me to marry my second wife.

How *wrong* I was. I *convinced* myself that The Lord had spoken to me about my second marriage. I even heard others telling me it was the will of God.

Pride Is A Task Master

Do we take the time to *know* the will of God when it comes to marrying someone? I am finally admitting it. Pride is our go-to when it comes to *admitting* wrongs in marriage and life.

"Pride goeth before destruction, and an haughty spirit before a fall," (Proverbs 16:18).

You can learn from my failures and know what it means in your life to hear the Voice of God. Do not allow pride to *overrule* God's Voice.

Have a clear direction and path to walk on. I went through *failures* because of my *selfish* wants and desires. That is why my second marriage was a *repetition* of my first.

Following God's Voice will *break* the cycle.

Chapter 11: He Does Not Know Your Plans.

My Ex-Wife Deserves Credit.

I want to applaud my ex-wife from my second marriage for being with me for over 17 years. That may sound strange, but it takes a great deal of faith to be espoused to someone you do not love.

Many marriages are like that today. My ex-wife *dared* to exit the marriage no matter who was affected because she was *hurting*. Her only recourse to her suffering was to divorce me, the *source* of her unhappiness.

In the United States, the court system generally makes it *easier* to divorce instead of trying to help *salvage* the marriage. The State of Louisiana has what it calls *covenant marriage*. It is not easy to go behind someone's back to get a divorce. I lived in that state for four years and even had the honor of performing marriage ceremonies which were an blessing to officiate.

Here is some information about Covenant Marriage in the State of Louisiana:

The couple who chooses to enter into a covenant marriage agrees to be bound by two significant provisions on obtaining a divorce or separation. These stipulations do not apply to other couples married in Louisiana:

1. The couple legally agrees to seek marital counseling if problems develop during the marriage; and

2. The couple can seek a divorce or legal separation for limited reasons only, as explained herein.

Declaration of Intent

In order to enter into a covenant marriage, the couple must sign a Declaration of Intent that provides:

1. A marriage agreement to live together as husband and wife forever;

2. The parties have chosen each other carefully and disclosed to each other "everything which could adversely affect" the decision to marry;

3. *The parties have received premarital counseling;*

4. *A commitment that if the parties experience marital difficulties they agree to make all reasonable efforts to preserve their marriage, including marital counseling; and*

5. *The couple also must obtain premarital counseling from a priest, minister, rabbi or similar clergyman of any religious sect, or from a professional marriage counselor.*

I Knew Something Was Wrong

You may *suspect* something is wrong. However, until you get blindsided, you never really know what to expect. I am sharing from my experience at the end of my second marriage. I *knew* we were having problems, but I never *expected* to be served divorce papers by my ex-wife on the day *after* our anniversary.

At 10 a.m., her plans for that day unfolded. She made her move. I cannot begin to express how my life changed that day. The woman I *loved* never loved me back and wanted *out* of the marriage. She had been living in *regret* all those years.

I pray this book gives you Hope for your marriage. I pray you give your marriage *another* chance to survive.

Many individuals who are served divorce papers are caught *unaware* and never put in the work necessary to save their marriage. There is *always* hope if you *look* for it. I know these are muddy waters, and you may believe your only remedy is divorce.

Pain and discomfort will cause you to make the *wrong* decision. If you listen to the wrong voices saying, "If I were you…" while knowing nothing about God's plan for your marriage, those bad influences would grossly *mislead* you.

How many will stand before God one day to give account for giving *bad* advice, like Job's friends? They knew nothing of *why* Job was in that situation. Read the Book of Job and see how God handled that situation. He turned it around to bless Job and his friends. You will be surprised how connected you are to Job.

Have You Given It Your Best?

If you know deep down inside, you have not given your *best* effort to save your marriage, step back, rethink, pray, and seek the mind of The Lord on your situation. Remember, God *hates* divorce. But, he will help you *save* your marriage.

God wanted to save my *first* marriage. It was never God's plan for me to marry again, only to go through *another* divorce. I live with that each day, knowing I let God down as a Leader in the Body of Christ. Yet I know He has *forgiven* me.

It takes two to agree to *fight* a good fight and *save* a marriage.

"For the Lord, the God of Israel, saith that He hateth putting away: for one covereth violence with his garment, saith the Lord of hosts: therefore take heed to your spirit, that ye deal not treacherously," (Malachi 2:16).

"Surely the Lord God will do nothing, but He revealeth His secret unto His servants the prophets," (Amos 3:7).

Deal Not Treacherously

The Collins English Dictionary states *Treachery is characterized by faithlessness or readiness to betray trust, traitorous.*

When you live *outside* the will of God, you are not in faith. Your feelings *dictate* you. When I filed for divorce at the end of my first marriage, my ex-wife and I had been *separated* for two years. I was seeing someone before our divorce was finalized. I was still *legally* married, yet I wrongly believed it was the will of God for me to move on with her.

God's Word is very clear. You need to begin to *look* at your marriage the way God views it. In His eyes, you are still married and not divorced. I was *wrong* to date someone while going through the divorce proceedings. During that time, I should have *fully* turned to His Word. Instead, I did not allow God to *seal* the wounds in my life from which I never healed.

Pain will cause you to make plans no matter who you hurt in the process. Hurt *keeps* on hurting others. Hurt people *hurt* people.

If you are in a domestic violence situation and you are *frightened* for your life, that is an issue that requires you to move to a *safe* place, especially if you have children. That is an escape plan I am fully in agreement with.

Who Is Speaking Into Your Life?

I have had ample time to look back and recognize how off track I was. I remember receiving a call from a false prophet. Back then, you could not have convinced me he was a *false* prophet. He described my second wife down to the *exact* length of her hair. He *insisted* she was the woman for me. He *affirmed* she was my wife and I was in the will of God.

How wrong I was!

I had not received my *final* divorce decree. I was *easily* deceived because I was far away from God. That is what sin will do. Sin *blinds* you to the disaster that awaits you.

Take a moment to be *honest* with yourself. Are you far away from God with sin in your life? If you are *willing* to repent, God will *restore* your heart.

"If we confess our sins, He is faithful and just to forgive us our sins, and to cleanse us from all unrighteousness," (1 John 1:9).

Are You Living In Peace?

Ask God to *examine* your heart to see if you are really in faith. Make sure you are not the reason for a less than peaceful relationship with your spouse. Do not allow *pride* to keep you from living peacefully and humbly. May God be your Guide.

"If it be possible, as much as liveth in you live peaceabley with all men," (Roman 12:18).

There will be some conflicts you *cannot* avoid. What is essential, *admit* the wrong you have done, and thereby *clear* the record. Do not plan to do *evil* to your spouse, especially when you know there is *hope* for your marriage.

My wife from my second marriage never asked me if I *wanted* a divorce from her. Likewise, I never asked my first wife if *she* wanted a divorce from me, even though she was in a relationship. From God's viewpoint, when the *head* of the household is off, everything else in the home will be *off-balance*.

Are you willing to admit the wrong you *contributed* to the failed marriage? Then, listen to God's Voice. He wants to help you and love you through it all.

The Seeds You Have Been Sowing

The following verses are very clear about what happens when you sow *bad* seeds.

"Be not deceived; God is not mocked: for whatsoever a man soweth, that shall he also reap. For he that soweth to his flesh shall of the flesh reap corruption; but he that soweth to the Spirit shall of the Spirit reap life everlasting. And let us not be weary in well doing: for in due season we shall reap, if we faint not," (Galatians 6:7-9).

Are you feeling *faint*? Have you given up on each other? Remember, God's Love will *always* find a way.

Nothing in your life will seem right until your *mind* is right. Someone may be properly advising you, but your mind is not right, and your spirit is all over the place. It is not the will of God for you to be in that state. If you are living in confusion on what you need to do, your decisions will *follow* suit. You will not make any *sound* decisions.

If a divorce is what you want, and you are not willing to take the words in this book as a *lifeline* to help your marriage, you are being led by the spirit of pride. The Bible teaches that pride comes before a fall.

"Pride goeth before destruction, and an haughty spirit before a fall," (Proverbs 16:18).

I hope you will learn from my mistakes, and *please save your marriage!*

Chapter 12: Escape Plans

There Is No Plan B!

Have you ever been invited to an event you never wanted to attend, especially an *after-work* function? Life put *unexpected* demands on you, and it may be something you do not want to be a part of.

So you figure out an *escape* plan.

I never thought anyone who wanted to be married would have an escape plan in the *back* of their mind. However, what is in a person's heart might *surprise* you during times of difficulty. Life is full of storms and trials that will *test* you, whether you are a believer or an unbeliever.

You would think the Body of Christ would have *zero-tolerance* when it comes to divorce. Numbers do not lie. Believers have about the *same* divorce rate as unbelievers when we should be the *hopeful* example of what the Lord can and will do to help marriages *stay* together.

If you go *into* marriage with an escape plan, your union is already *doomed*. Only the Lord can *change* your heart. The only way that can happen is by you being honest with yourself. I hope my book *stops* your marriage from heading to Divorce Court. Instead, I desire for my book to be a *lifeline* for your marriage that will lead you to the Hope you have in Christ.

"For as he thinketh in his heart, so is he: Eat and drink, saith he to thee; but his heart is not with thee," (Proverbs 23:7).

Make A Commitment

This verse *emphasizes* the importance of your heart. If your heart is not *genuinely* committed to the one you are with, you will just go through the motions for all the *wrong* reasons. Some people marry for money or because their suitor has a good job that will *provide* everything they want in life. Shift from the escape plan mindset and *commit* to loving your spouse with all your heart.

I have been married *twice*. That is nothing to be proud of. My only hope now is to stand at the wall of hope and pull you out of any bad decisions before it is too late. May my failure help you *find* your way back to restoration.

Do not allow the enemy to make you think all hope is *lost*. *Please Help Me Save My Marriage!* was written for you. Not just to read, but to *apply* in your life. When I go to church, I expect a word that will *challenge* my faith and help me become a *better* person and *stronger* man of faith.

Everyone experiences some form of failure in life. You can emerge victoriously. If this is your first marriage, you do not want to look back one day and say, "I have been divorced several times."

The only person that needs to get it together is you. If you remember, Sister Becky Kline asked God to *touch* her heart. Once that happened, Brother Kline changed. God began a work in their hearts that gives hope to other couples who need a word of encouragement.

Do Not Remain In Harm's Way

If you are in a domestic situation and your life is being *threatened*, you need to get out now while you have a *chance* to live. It is not God's will for someone to be beating you.

If you have been hit *once*, that is once *too* much. I am not saying a person cannot change. However, looking at the numbers on domestic abuse in our society, you should get out *now*, especially if your children witness your abuse. If you cannot live as a couple together peaceably, God's Word is very clear on what to do.

"If it be possible, as much as lieth in you, live peaceably with all men.

"Dearly beloved, avenge not yourselves, but rather give place unto wrath: for it is written, Vengeance is Mine; I will repay, saith the Lord.

"Therefore if thine enemy hunger, feed him; if he thirst, give him drink: for in so doing thou shalt heap coals of fire on his head.

"Be not overcome of evil, but overcome evil with good," (Romans 12:18-21).

Your Life Is Worth Living

I cannot even imagine how it feels to lay down at night knowing the person you are lying down next to is abusing you in some way. Please get out because your life is worth living. God loves you and will help you to recover.

If you are not in an abusive marriage, I will encourage you to give your marriage a chance. There are many resources available to help you recover. Chances are, the person you want to escape from prefers to *save* the marriage if you give them a chance.

The Klines suggested a retreat for couples. A retreat could be your destination for help and support. Do not allow pride to keep you from admitting you *need* help. Pride can keep you in *bondage* because you are *unwilling* to acknowledge that your marriage is in *trouble* and you need help.

Do not give up on the other person. I have been through the pain of divorce *twice*. It is not a pretty picture. I hope to help others fight the good fight to *save* their marriage. I gave up on my first marriage too soon. If I fought one more day and believed God, we would have *overcome* the struggles we were going through. We would have *remained* united.

Sometime after my first wife and I separated, I remember meeting her at a Kroger store about 30 miles from where we once lived. I asked her to give our marriage another chance, but she turned me down.

What is important is that you can look back one day and say that you gave your marriage your *best* effort. Your marriage is *worth* it. Then, when escape plans are no longer part of your thoughts, you can set yourself up for victory.

Chapter 13: The Invisible Enemy Attacking Your Marriage

Some Enemies Are Hidden.

As I was writing this book, we were smack dab in the middle of the COVID-19 pandemic in America and worldwide. Many lives have been *lost* to the virus.

President Donald Trump called it the *invisible* enemy that started in a Chinese lab. We never knew in advance how to *prepare* ourselves for what was coming. But, at some point, we were *required* to wear a mask everywhere we went, even to Church.

In your marriage, you can be attacked on your *blindside* and never see it coming.

The question is, can you learn from a brother who has been divorced *twice* in his lifetime? You cannot *afford* a day *off* when it comes to your marriage. If I think I did everything *right*, I can still look back and realize that I *failed* in both my marriages. It was never God's plan for me to be a *victim* of divorce.

The invisible enemy came in and caused *division* in my household. Instead of seeking out counsel that would *challenge* me and not merely agree with me, I surrounded myself with individuals that were an echo of what I *wanted* to hear. I was not *willing* to listen to the *truth* about my first marriage nor my second.

Saying I have been married twice is nothing I am proud of; that is why I hope you will *conquer* the invisible *intruder* wreaking havoc in your household and marriage. The counsel you are allowing into your spirit will either *keep* you from hearing God or draw you *closer* to Him. Only by hearing from God will your efforts be on point and precise.

Have You Noticed The Signs?

We were in a storm in America. The world around us was sharing in the same pandemic. Lives were being *lost*. Social distancing was a part of *everyday* life. On the days I ventured out, I observed the signs on the floors of stores and places of business, reminding us that social distancing was *required* to stop this pandemic.

I wonder how many marriages are in *deeper* trouble due to this pandemic. The invisible enemy was already at work in many hearts *before* the pandemic started. It may have caused many to give up.

"When a strong man armed keepeth his palace, his goods are in peace: But when a stronger than he shall come upon him, and overcome him, he taketh from him all his armour wherein he trusted, and divideth his spoils," (Luke 11:21-22).

The enemy is always *looking* for your *weak* points. That is why it is important to *discern* who you are talking with and *sharing* your marital problems with. A wrong person can take *advantage* of your weakness and try coming in to destroy what you have spent many years laboring to build.

How come it is *easier* to trust God to *bless* you in many ways, yet it seems like the *last* person you want to *consult* is God?

The Transformed Life

A transformed *life* should reflect a transformed *marriage*. Consider these questions as they apply in your life.

Why do you stop *trusting* God...when it comes to your marriage?

Why do you stop trusting God...when it comes to *healing* your hearts?

Why do you stop trusting God...when you hear sound *wisdom* and only want to listen to what makes you feel *good*?

Why do you stop trusting God...when it comes to staying *together,* which will, in turn, *glorify* Him and bless others because they will see His *faithfulness* through your marriage?

Why do you stop trusting God...when it comes your *marriage*, yet you trust Him with all your other needs?

You have faith in God for everything else *except* your marriage. *Why?* You stopped trusting God because of pride, which ultimately produces self-righteousness in your heart.

If you only think of yourself and not the other person willing to do what it takes, why not *change* and give your marriage a chance? Do not allow the *invisible* enemy of your soul to keep you from God's very best.

"Or despisest thou the riches of His goodness and forbearance and longsuffering; not knowing that the goodness of God leadeth thee to repentance?" (Roman 2:4).

"If we confess our sins, He is faithful and just to forgive us our sins, and to cleanse us from all unrighteousness," (1 John 1:9).

God is *for* both of you. He *wants* your marriage to work out. That is why I believe this book is a message to help encourage you not to give up. Instead, be *committed* to seeing the victory you have in Christ.

Remember, you cannot *afford* to have a day *off* concerning your marriage. Express love and commitment. Give each other *heartfelt* assurance. Pray for each other *every* day. That will make a difference in *building* each other up and keeping the oil *burning* with love, something vitally important to your relationship.

Chapter 14: Do Not Ask Your Neighbor

Tell Your Neighbor!

What goes through your mind when you go to particular ministries and are told to give your neighbor a high five in agreement with what is being said?

Your neighbor may not know what you are going through at the moment. So for me to give them a high five seems like a *waste* of energy and time because I need a word that will *build* my faith instead of high fives every few minutes.

That is the problem you may face. Unfortunately, you are playing patty cake and asking the *wrong* individuals to help with your marital issues. As a result, you are *wasting* energy and will continue to be disappointed because you are *off* course.

Your questions will depend on your belief system. Based on that belief system, you make decisions *each* day. Everything you do is *governed* by it. For example, did God allow what happened, or did you *position* yourself for what happened to you?

Is the only way you can handle the outcome to *blame* God by saying He *allowed* it to happen and you had *nothing* to do with it? *Be honest.* What happened to Job in The Bible was because God *allowed* it to happen for a *purpose.*

Who Did You Blame?

Do you blame God every time something happens in your life? Yet, God had *nothing* to do with your decisions. Going *outside* of God's plan will cause heartache. Have you been impatient and taken matters into your own hands *without* inner peace and direction?

This verse will help you to understand what happens when you go outside the will of God. "For the rod of the wicked shall not rest upon the lot of the righteous; lest the righteous put forth their hands unto iniquity," (Psalm 125:3).

Look at the very beginning of your relationship *before* your crisis started. Take inventory and be completely honest.

Your decision to *follow* God will require a *total* heart commitment to Him and obedience. As a pastor, I can honestly say I saw a big *difference* between those who did not submit to the will of God and those who *did*.

Many believers who are not fully committed to the Lord will be *challenged* during the growing pains of their faith. When you are the only person in the marriage *seeking* God and *growing* in faith, it will either pull you as a couple together or apart. That is why God's Word teaches us not to be *unequally* yoked.

"Be ye not unequally yoked together with unbelievers: for what fellowship hath righteousness with unrighteousness? and what communion hath light with darkness?" (2 Corinthians 6:14).

The Unbelieving Couple

If you are in a marriage where *neither* person was saved but *later* decided to give their heart to the Lord, God has a word of encouragement for you. When your faith is *challenged* during the hard times, you will find out who is with you. There is a reason why God said let no man *separate* whoever He put together.

"What therefore God hath joined together, let not man put asunder," (Mark 10:9).

"For the unbelieving husband is sanctified by the wife, and the unbelieving wife is sanctified by the husband: else were your children unclean; but now are they holy. But if the unbelieving depart, let him depart. A brother or a sister is not under bondage in such cases: but God hath called us to peace," (1 Corinthians 7:14-15).

While we were pastoring, we had a *Toolbox for Marriage* ministry. We had the *first* meeting in our home. My stepson helped me decorate the toolboxes. We filled them with books and materials for assisting marriages.

Our goal was to meet *once* a month with words of encouragement and healing. But, unfortunately, we did all this not knowing our marriage was in *trouble* and headed to Divorce Court.

Is God In It?

My second marriage was not what it *needed* to be. Only God's mercy could have helped us work through the difficult times. I remember telling everyone it was the will of God for me to marry her, when in reality, God had *nothing* to do with it. So now the question is, could our marriage have been saved?

Absolutely, *yes*, if two believers would have *agreed* to do what needed to be done!

God will bless you and turn your marriage around. Please do not make the *mistake* many couples make and just give up. I want you to succeed where many have *failed* to trust God.

Remember, God *hates* divorce.

"For the Lord, the God of Israel, saith that he hateth putting away: for one covereth violence with his garment, saith the Lord of hosts: therefore take heed to your spirit, that ye deal not treacherously," (Malachi 2:16).

I *know* God has *forgiven* me for my failed marriages. However, it *hurts* my heart to know I *disappointed* God by not fighting to *save* my marriages.

After my second divorce, I looked back over my life and realized I could have done *more*. That is my message to you as you read this book. I hope you will *awaken* to the fact that there is *more* you can do. Asking the *wrong* person for help causes you to look back with *regret* and *disappointment*.

Ask The Right Person!

You will not get to the truth until you ask the *right* person. Before any problem can be solved, you must *first* talk with the source. I know you have your best friends you believe *know* you.

The question is, do *you* know you?

Is it possible to *confront* yourself? Who knows you *better* than you? You know *why* you do the things that you do.

Be *honest* with yourself.

You can *sabotage* your future by doing things that cause significant pain and damage to yourself and others. You can *solve* your problems *without* asking your neighbors because you *already* know the answer. What did you do Yesterday to get the results you are facing Today? You can do a lot of things to yourself, thinking you are *protecting* the outcome.

When I look back over my life and reevaluate the outcome of my *failed* marriages, I can genuinely say I *allowed* the wrong individuals to *speak* into my life.

Until you are willing to *admit* where you failed, you will continue to *flounder* throughout your life without fulfilling your purpose according to God's plan for your life and wellbeing.

Who Has Your Ear?

After my first wife and I separated, I remember going to visit my mother. She mentioned she had a friend that was *interested* in me. That experience turned out to be a life lesson for me to understand better the decisions I was facing.

My mother went on to say that this lady was *also* going through a divorce. The lady wanted my mother to introduce her to me. My mother *adamantly* refused.

When I asked why she said the lady was *over* 80 and going through her *sixth* divorce. I could not believe that an 80-year-old lady thought I would be *interested* in her.

I needed to *learn* from my past and *stop* allowing the *wrong* people to speak into my life. My mother was not the wrong person. She was my *protector,* and she *loved* me. Only God and a godly person will understand the pain you are going through. When you need a *straight* answer, they may not always *agree* with you, though what they tell you will be to your *advantage* at the end of the day.

Who Knows You Best?

Who knows you *better* than you?

Here is where you need to be completely honest if you want *real* change. Here is where you can *sabotage* the outcome if you are not genuine.

Do you *love* yourself and *what* you have become? I am talking about the self only *you* can see.

Hollywood need not look far because some of us are good actors and deserve an Academy Award!

Do not ask your neighbor. The Bible instructs you to *love* your neighbor as yourself. "Honour thy father and thy mother: and, Thou shalt love thy neighbor as thyself," (Matthew 19:19).

Love Your Neighbor As Yourself

The Lord may have commanded us to *love* your neighbor as yourself, but you are not obligated to *consult* them.

Look in the mirror and start being *true* to yourself, the man or woman you were created to be. Once you start *loving* yourself and being *thankful* because you are a gift to your mate and others, then and only then will you *appreciate* your worth. Consequently, things will start turning around in your life.

When you begin to *love* right, you will ask the right *person,* and you will be *ready* to receive correction and love.

You may be wondering about my former wives and the *pain* they were going through. You may even be asking *how* they are doing today? I often wonder.

My first wife was very *kind* at the end of our divorce proceedings. I *regret* giving up too soon. I believe if I had waited *one* more day and not given up on us, we would be *together* today. But, unfortunately, I was *always* trying to *restore* the marriage, then I became *weary* of well-doing and gave up.

Sometimes your pain can be so *deep* you do not have the words to *express* what you are enduring.

I Became Weary

When my first wife realized I was not going back to her, and it was *truly* over, she *tried* to bring us back together. I had never seen that happen before. But, as I stated earlier, I had become *weary* and decided to move on with my second wife.

What a *mistake* that was. Oh, the *suffering* we went through for 17 years! Yet, we did have *bright* spots of prosperity and spiritual growth. Nevertheless, with the wrong neighbors influencing our lives, I ended up welcoming divorce once again.

What Job went through was God's plan. But, unfortunately, many times, what we go through is *our* plan and *will* fail.

I have an assignment for you.

Read the Book of Job. The request was made to God by Satan concerning Job's life. As a result, God let down His hedge of protection that surrounded Job so that he would *demonstrate* another side of his *commitment* to serving God. How *wrong* satan was about his character.

You will enjoy and value Job's commitment to his faith, even when his wife *incited* him to curse God and die.

"And he took him a potsherd to scrape himself withal, and he sat down among the ashes. Then said his wife unto him, Dost thou still retain thine integrity? curse God, and die. But he said unto her, Thou speakest as one of the foolish women speaketh. What? shall we receive good at the hand of God, and shall we not receive evil? In all this did not Job sin with his lips," (Job 2:8-10).

You can appreciate how Job stood *alone*. Even his friends misunderstood what he was going through.

The Right One Matters

As this chapter comes to a close, I will not leave you hanging concerning Job's wife. Instead, let me share some insight. It is *essential* to be with the right one in life.

When you are *down*, you will find out if the person you are with has *stopped* believing in you and wants you to throw in the towel and give up on the marriage and life.

It is important to keep *building* up your faith. As the days go by, you will need faith in God that will give you *discernment* to know who to open yourself up to *before* you share your heart.

Obey God, and your *outcome* will bring Him all the glory. Whether you remain together or stay apart, you will *know* you have done God's will. May your marriage be *healed* to the glory of God.

If you are not a believer, I hope you will decide to *accept* Christ in your life. At the end of this book, you will find the Plan of Salvation to give you a deeper understanding of starting a relationship with Christ.

Until then, be *encouraged* by these verses. They have brought me great *comfort* during some difficult times.

"For God is not the Author of confusion, but of peace, as in all churches of the saints," (1 Corinthians 14:33).

"Beloved, believe not every spirit, but try the spirits whether they are of God:

because many false prophets are gone out into the world," (1 John 4:1).

"Give therefore Thy servant an understanding heart to judge Thy people, that I may discern between good and bad: for who is able to judge this Thy so great a people?" (1 Kings 3:9).

"For the word of God is quick, and powerful, and sharper than any twoedged sword, piercing even to the dividing asunder of soul and spirit, and of the joints and marrow, and is a discerner of the thoughts and intents of the heart," (Hebrews 4:12).

Chapter 15: I Know What You Have Been Told

We Need Each Other.

Why would someone tell you it is *best* to be alone and do your *own* thing? God never meant for us to be alone. We *need* each other.

I have interviewed a few ladies with this question. Before you got married, what good and bad advice was given to you?

Let us start with the *good* advice.

Once you are married, a woman may have been instructed to *love* her husband and make sure he is *well* cared for. Wash and clean his clothes. While you are at it, if you have time, wash your clothes and the children's.

I saw nothing wrong with this advice until I read Proverbs 31:10. That woman goes way beyond that advice and *adds* so much more to the marriage.

"Who can find a virtuous woman? for her price is far above rubies," (Proverbs 31:10).

You can be *all* that The Lord has called you to be.

It is not too late for the light to come on and start in the direction that will bring more *life* to your marriage. I am not saying it is God's will for *everyone* to be married. But, you should know in *your* heart if that is a desire you have.

"And the Lord God said, It is not good that the man should be alone; I will make him an help meet for him," (Genesis 2:18).

Marriage Is Honorable

It is not good for man and woman to be alone. Marriage is God's plan for life. I have been married *twice,* with both marriages ending in divorce. That is nothing to be proud of. I wear it as a badge of dishonor. My mission is to help married couples *avoid* Divorce Court.

I know what it is to feel *alone*. During my second marriage, I would cry out and ask God why I felt so alone. You may be going through that now and wondering if it will be like this all the time. But, if you want things to change, you will have to put on the armor described in the Book of Ephesians.

"Put on the whole armour of God, that ye may be able to stand against the wiles of the devil," (Ephesians 6:11).

You have an enemy, and the only way to have victory over your enemy is to *focus* on God's Word and not your problems. Seek godly help through counseling, couples' retreats, Bible study together, and maybe watch a marriage building series together. We have many resources to help you get past this pain. If you want your marriage to work, all it takes is an effort with determination and the Love of God.

Beware of Bad Marriage Advice

Let me address the *bad* advice.

If the marriage does not work, get out while you can because it is *best* to be single, so you will not have someone *ordering* you around.

Many individuals think marriage is all about being ordered around. That may be true in some cultures. However, that is not what is prescribed in God's Word. The Proverbs 31 woman's voice was *heard*. The marketplace knew her husband because of her.

"Who can find a virtuous woman? for her price is far above rubies. The heart of her husband doth safely trust in her, so that he shall have no need of spoil. She will do him good and not evil all the days of her life," (Proverbs 31:10-12).

"Her husband is known in the gates, when he sitteth among the elders of the land," (Proverbs 31:23).

"She openeth her mouth with wisdom; and in her tongue is the law of kindness," (Proverbs 31: 26).

My next assignment for you is to read the whole of Proverbs 31, especially verses 10-31.

That chapter is very clear about a woman's role in the marriage. The Kline and the Williams families are lovely examples of that. So many can look to them for hope. Each wife has a *voice* in their marriage, and they are beautiful examples of what Proverbs 31 teaches us.

A Trap Called Tradition

The traditions of man make the Word of God of no effect. When people add their marriage philosophies to God's Word, they make life *unbearable,* and neither partner can *fulfill* their purpose.

When The Word of God is *tainted* by tradition, those who receive the teaching miss out on the benefit of the Power of The Word working on their behalf. Only when we get back to God's Word in marriage can each person fulfill their role.

"Making the word of God of none effect through your tradition, which ye have delivered: and many such like things do ye," (Mark 7:13).

Remember the movie, *History of The World,* when Mel Brooks came down from the mountain as Moses carrying three tablets and said, "The Lord Jehovah has given these 15 Commandments."

He accidentally *drops* one of the tablets and quickly *corrects* himself, "Ten...Ten Commandments!"

This is what happens when we do not understand God's Word concerning marriage. We end up *misquoting* God's plan and directions. It is time to step up so healing can come to your *entire* family.

A Word For Men

Brother Kline discerned the spiritual condition of his family and his wife's heart desire. Sir, you are the head of your household. *Do you know the spiritual temperature in your home and what is needed to bring healing to your loved ones?*

Who gave you advice on how you should *lead* your family? I was trained by men who did not provide sound advice on being a godly man in my household. I was told to be at Church 24/7 because church came *before* the family.

One day, I woke up and knew that was not true. Unfortunately, the damage was *already* done, and our relationship never recovered.

I have *chosen* to be truthful, vulnerable, and transparent about my past so that you can relate and minister to your family before it is too late.

Do not let pride *stop* you from saving your family. "Pride goeth before destruction, and an haughty spirit before a fall," (Proverbs 16:18).

Wake Up Before It Is Too Late!

Chapter 16: Hopefully, A Change of Heart

Change Is Proof of Life.

How many times have you heard someone say, "This is just the way I am, and I will never change?"

Think about all the changes we go through in life.

Age changes us. *Health* changes us. *Seasons* change. *People* change. *Nature* changes. *Climate* changes. *Prices* always fluctuate. *Gas* prices seem to change daily.

After pastoring and sitting across the desk from the haves and the have nots, I have seen a difference in those *committed* to changing and making life *better* for themselves and their loved ones and those who are not.

I know couples who are going through the same vicious cycle because they are *stuck* in pride-producing self-righteousness.

During my first marriage, I remember my first wife telling me I *knew* how she was *before* I married her. That was true. However, if you are not *willing* to change to make life better, that is *pride*.

"Pride goeth before destruction, and an haughty spirit before a fall," (Proverbs 16:18).

After going through two divorces and pastoring, I have a wealth of knowledge to share to assist those who want help and desire to *avoid* the pain of divorce. I have *rebuilt* my life twice. That is the season I am in now. I am rebuilding and hoping for a *better* future.

I Want To Be Married Again

I cannot believe I *want* to be married again. Well, I do. I know the importance of a *heart* change and *learning* from my past, so my future will be *better*. I am not giving up on the institution of marriage. I believe my *future* wife is *waiting* for me to find her. It will be an excellent *match*.

Please Help Me Save My Marriage! was written to give you hope and the realization it will take a heart *change* to *save* your marriage. If, by chance, you are not a Christian, this would be an excellent time to learn about the Savior.

At the end of this chapter, I will leave the *Plan of Salvation* with Scriptures to help you know why it is essential to have Christ in your heart. He will help you face what you are up against in this season of change. You can become a new creature in Christ Jesus.

"Therefore if any man be in Christ, he is a new creature: old things are passed away; behold, all things are become new," (2 Corinthians 5:17).

If you are a believer, but you are *fighting* the change that The Lord *requires*, you need to check your salvation to see if you are a believer.

Salvation is all about change.

Transformation.

"And be not conformed to this world: but be ye transformed by the renewing of your mind, that ye may prove what is that good, and acceptable, and perfect, will of God," (Romans 12:2).

The Willing Heart

Embracing change takes a willing heart that only The Lord Jesus Christ can *form* in those who will come to Him and *repent* of their sins. You have to be ready to become *more* like Christ. Saving your marriage will take a heart change. Your willing heart will keep you out of Divorce Court.

If you have prayed about other things that have happened in your life and God answered, why is it so hard to *trust* God with your marriage? What is more important than your well-being and family?

Why *replace* your wife or husband with someone else? How can you even pray about being with someone *else* when you are *already* married? Do not get it twisted. God will not ordain you to marry someone else while you are still married. I do not care how good it *feels* to your flesh.

If you are an unbeliever and you are about to exit your marriage so you can be with someone else, thinking things will get better, God's Word states, it rains on the just and the unjust.

None of us will get away with doing wrong. "That ye may be the children of your Father Which is in heaven: for He maketh his sun to rise on the evil and on the good, and sendeth rain on the just and on the unjust," (Matthew 5:45).

Rebuilding Is Not Easy

Economically, a man tends to lose so much more from a divorce. It takes several years to recover. Children are witnesses to the *struggles* of the rebuilding process. If you factor in the divorce rates, you will understand why so many are *hesitant* to marry.

After a divorce happens, it hurts everyone involved, *especially* children. When children become a part of that equation and *witness* the damage from the aftermath, they too become *discouraged* about marriage or *subconsciously* sabotage any good relationship they may have.

Change Your Attitude

A change of heart will help you *alter* your outlook. God *answers* prayers. He will *comfort* you.

Pride kept me from fighting for my first marriage. I *allowed* my feelings to get in the way. My first wife had started seeing someone after a season of separation. I should have stepped in *before* all that happened. Instead, I decided divorce was the answer.

How *wrong* I was.

My *sons* loved me.

My *daughter* loved me as well.

However, when I think about the time *lost* and the *damaged* relationships, it was not worth it. I needed a *change* of heart. You do too. Your recovery will require a *different* approach.

If you do *everything* possible to save your marriage and it does not work out, at least you can look back one day *knowing* you did not just give up without a *righteous* fight. Your legacy will *speak* for you. Someone will witness the fact you did not give up without making an effort.

Unlocking The Best For Your Life

The padlock below indicates a *combination* of the daily events that need to happen within your heart to move your life *forward.*

Saying "Yes" to all these areas *unlocks* God's best for your life.

Faith	**Yes** —	Love
Joy	**Yes** —	Forgiveness
Longsuffering	— **Yes** —	Forbearance
Gentleness	— **Yes** —	Kindness
Goodness	— **Yes** —	Honesty
Temperance	— **Yes** —	Meekness
	Patience	

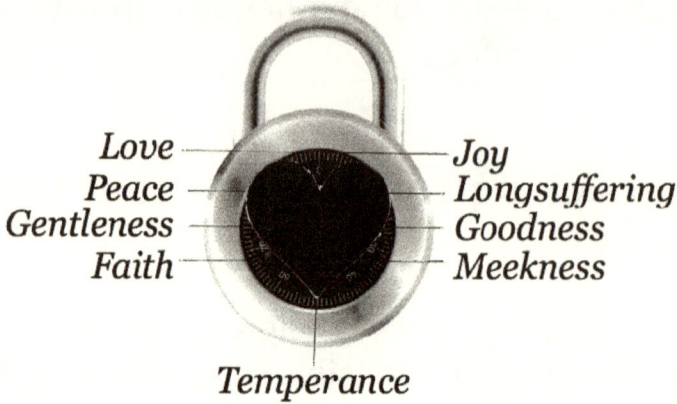

Love — Joy
Peace — Longsuffering
Gentleness — Goodness
Faith — Meekness

Temperance

"I can do all things through Christ Which strengthens me," (Philippians 4:13).

Forgive Someone

Your moving forward will always *start* with you *forgiving* someone. Only then will you be on the road to *recovery*. The image illustrates the *combination* of events that need to take place in our hearts at all times to *unlock* God's very best when needed. Only God's Power can open what has been *secured* in our hearts.

Take a look at this Scripture. "If ye be willing and obedient ye shall eat the good of the land," (Isaiah 1:19).

This verse is clear on what it will take to experience God's very best. A *willingness* to obey God in *every* area of your life will make you free *indeed* and give you the freedom to live.

"If the Son therefore shall make you free, ye shall be free indeed," (John 8:36).

This Scripture *speaks* to my heart because I am *free* indeed. A change of heart will free *you* as well. That is God's plan for you and the one you need to forgive. But, unfortunately, you may still be in a place where you do not see any way out but to divorce. That is *manipulation* by the enemy of your soul.

The Lord Wants To Set You Free

Make the list below a part of your *daily* devotion.

It will help you stay focused on *building* your faith and trust in the Lord. As you develop this daily habit, it is also an opportune time to begin walking in the combination of God's Love and Power so you can *receive* the freedom you truly need.

Perhaps your heart is like the *unopened* lock in the previous image. Do you know *why* you are on *lockdown*? Do you know the *personal* number it will take to *open* your heart like the lock below?

Love — Joy
Peace — Longsuffering
Goodness — Goodness
Faith — Meekness

Temperance

Once you open your heart, with the aid of The Holy Spirit, you can begin to operate *entirely* in the will of God, loving others as you should.

Faith	*Love*
Joy	*Forgiving*
Peace	*Forbearance*
Longsuffering	*Kindness*
Gentleness	*Honesty*
Goodness	*Meekness*
Temperance	*Patience*

The combination of the decisions indicated above is to be in play *always* in our life so that we can *unlock* God's very best.

"But the fruit of the Spirit is love, joy, peace, long-suffering, gentleness, goodness, faith, Meekness, temperance: against such there is no law," (Galatians 5:22-23).

8 Suggestions For Your Encouragement

"If it be possible, as much as lieth in you, live peaceably with all men," (Romans 12:18).

These action steps will *encourage* and *build* you both up so new life can flow into your hearts.

- Surround yourselves with individuals that are in *healthy* relationships.
- Choose to love *unconditionally* without limitations.
- Minister God's love as if your spouse's happiness is more *important* than your own.
- Put your relationship *ahead* of everyone and everything, including your children and any outside influence that is not helping you build.
- Go back to the *beginning* and start over from *scratch* and remember *why* you both fell in love.
- It is *essential* to stop taking one another for granted.
- Pray *fervently* for your spouse's wellbeing.

- It is crucial to seek out godly *counseling* and have the heart to *receive* it.

The End

Resources

Marriage

https://www.bettermarriagestx.org/

https://www.hopefortheheart.org/keys-for-living/

Domestic Abuse

https://www.thehotline.org/

It is not God's will for someone to cause you harm. The information above is to help you contact someone that can help you.

I know it is hard to believe, but men go through domestic abuse as well. The two links above will help in a crisis.

God's Plan For Your Life

Source: GotQuestion.com

Jesus paid the price for your salvation. The most important thing to understand about the Plan of Salvation is that it is God's plan, not humanity's plan.

Humanity's plan of salvation would be observing religious rituals or obeying specific commands, or achieving certain levels of spiritual enlightenment. But none of these things are part of God's Plan of Salvation.

God's Plan of Salvation:
The Why

In God's Plan of Salvation, first, we must understand why we need to be saved. Simply put, we need to be saved because we have sinned. The Bible declares that everyone has sinned (Ecclesiastes 7:20; Romans 3:23; 1 John 1:8).

Sin is rebellion against God. We all choose to do wrong things actively. Sin harms others, damages us, and, most importantly, dishonors God. The Bible also teaches that because God is holy and just, He cannot allow sin to go unpunished. The punishment for sin is death (Romans 6:23) and eternal separation from God (Revelation 20:11–15).

Without God's Plan of Salvation, eternal death is the destiny of every human being.

God's Plan of Salvation: The What

In God's Plan of Salvation, God Himself is the Only One Who can provide for our salvation. We are utterly unable to save ourselves because of our sin and its consequences.

God became a human being in the Person of Jesus Christ (John 1:1, 14). Jesus lived a sinless life (2 Corinthians 5:21; Hebrews 4:15; 1 John 3:5) and offered

Himself as a Perfect Sacrifice on our behalf (1 Corinthians 15:3; Colossians 1:22; Hebrews 10:10).

Since Jesus is God, His death was of infinite and eternal value. The death of Jesus Christ on The Cross fully paid for the entire world's sins (1 John 2:2). His Resurrection from the dead demonstrated that His Sacrifice was indeed sufficient and that salvation is now available.

God's Plan of Salvation: The How

In Acts 16:31, a man asked the Apostle Paul how to be saved. Paul's response was, "Believe in the Lord Jesus Christ, and you will be saved."

The way to follow God's Plan of Salvation is to believe. That is the only requirement (John 3:16; Ephesians 2:8–9).

God has provided for our salvation through Jesus Christ. All we must do is receive it, by faith, fully trusting in Jesus alone as Savior (John 14:6; Acts 4:12).

That is God's Plan of Salvation.

God's Plan of Salvation:
Will You Receive It?

If you are ready to follow God's Plan of Salvation, place your faith in Jesus as your Savior. Change your mind from embracing sin and rejecting God to rejecting sin and embracing God through Jesus Christ.

Fully trust in the sacrifice of Jesus as the perfect and complete payment for your sins. If you do this, God's Word promises that you will be saved. God will forgive your sins. You will spend eternity in Heaven.

There is no more important decision.

Place your faith in Jesus Christ as your Savior today!

My Personal Email Address

DonaldSmithTX@gmail.com

About The Author

Donald W Smith is the President of *Time for Results Coaching* located in Fort Worth, Texas. He is the founder and former Senior Pastor of *Harvest Church* and has had the honor of serving his community in that position for over twelve years.

Donald W Smith is the author of his first book *Forgive Who? How A Man Can Forgive His Ex-Wife And Move On With His Life.* He has also written a book *What's Love Got To Do With It? Everything!*

Donald W Smith received his *Associate of Arts in Theological and Ministerial Studies* from Tyndale Theology Bible College of Fort Worth, Texas. He also received his *Master of Divinity in Theology, Marriage and Family Therapy/Counseling* from Christian Bible College of Louisiana in 2002.

www.ingramcontent.com/pod-product-compliance
Lightning Source LLC
La Vergne TN
LVHW011328080426
835513LV00006B/242